"*The Power of the 72* is a breath of fresh air, it injects much-needed life into what unfortunately has become the stale church practice of evangelism. John Teter expresses passion and joy through this text that encourages readers toward a holistic and healthy approach to sharing the power of the gospel message."

Soong-Chan Rah, Milton B. Engebretson Professor of Church Growth and Evangelism, North Park Theological Seminary

"Having modeled to them what his kingdom looks like, Jesus sent seventy-two vulnerable people out into all the towns and villages, endowed with his authority, to alert everyone to his marvelous reign and rule. It was a kind of beautiful, organized chaos. John Teter thinks we can't improve on it. After all, he and his church have been doing it this way for years. Developing his approach based on Luke 10, John presents an inspiring and readable vision for missional evangelism the Jesus way."

Michael Frost, author of *Surprise the World!* and *To Alter Your World*

"John Teter knows his stuff. He has been one of the seventy-two, and he has also equipped literally thousands of the seventy-two: 'normal' church members. This book will impact your prayer life, your sense of calling, your view of Scripture, and how you see urban America. It's dripping with good news, rooted in real stories ranging from Starbucks to former gang members. Brand new believers and church planters alike will be blessed by this read."

Doug Schaupp, national director of evangelism, InterVarsity Christian Fellowship/USA, coauthor of *Breaking the Huddle*

"Starting with a dozen Galilean men and a few women, Jesus expanded his ministry to the nations by commissioning seventy-two additional unnamed disciples to join his ministry team. In his new book, my good friend Pastor John Teter unpacks how embracing *The Power of the 72* can revolutionize our ability to impact our communities with the good news of the kingdom."

Noel Castellanos, president, Christian Community Development Association; author, *Where the Cross Meets the Street*

"John Teter's profound gift of transforming the intuitive to the intentional is never more evident than in *The Power of the 72.* He has taken our call for evangelism to another dimension with powerful and moving narratives from his life, family, church, and ministry experiences. Within this narrative flow, John then practically advises us to engage biblically, theologically, and experientially with becoming one of the seventy-two who were sent out by Jesus in Luke 10. This is without question the most engaging and comprehensive book on evangelism I have read. It is no surprise I finished reading it in one sitting—it was that compelling. This is a must-read for every Christian and every church."

Randall Y. Furushima, president emeritus, Pacific Rim Christian University, Honolulu, Hawaii

"Evangelism is a must for all Christians. Through this book, Dr. John Teter has provided not only biblical insight into the subject but also has offered valuable and practical suggestions on how to do it well. As John and his team have been helping us in Hong Kong with evangelism and church planting during the past few years, we really wish that this practical guide had arrived earlier."

Simon Yeung, honorary executive secretary, Mission Covenant Church, Hong Kong

"Pastor John put together a wonderful resource on evangelism for us in *The Power of 72*. He weaves personal stories with biblical exposition from Luke 10 forming a tapestry of wisdom for us to consider as we put our faith in motion. Dive in to the Word of God and let it simmer as you ruminate on his suggestions for reaching the world next door. You'll learn a lot along the way and may grow into a fruitful voice with Christ as you step out and practice what he teaches."

Joseph W. Handley Jr., president, Asian Access, Tokyo, Japan

"I've had the privilege of witnessing how God is at work at Fountain of Life Covenant Church in Long Beach, CA. This is a blueprint on how they have reached across race and class to make disciples of all people. People from all walks of life are being transformed and raised up as leaders. This book captures some of these incredible stories. Prepare to be challenged and to re-examine how your church can truly reach your wider community. Move beyond your fears or discomforts and imagine how God might use you and your community to make an impact, just like the 72."

Miho Buccholtz, copastor, Tokyo Life Church, Tokyo, Japan

"Sometimes in focusing on evangelism, we lose our focus on discipleship. Or if we focus on discipleship, we lose the evangelistic fervor. In his book *The Power of the 72*, John Teter challenges us with the importance of evangelism and provides practical application for every disciple to be sent out with power."

Dave Ferguson, lead pastor, Community Christian Church, Naperville, IL; author of *Finding Your Way Back to God* and *Starting Over*

"Over twenty years ago, the Lord brought me and John Teter together amid a sea of twenty thousand people. I have mentored, encouraged, and watched John consistently grow in his personal witness and evangelism leadership. In his new book, *The Power of the 72*, John combines insights from Luke 10, real stories from the frontlines of a church plant, and theories that he has been testing for years. I highly recommend this resource to develop evangelists in your ministry."

Alexander Gee Jr., senior pastor, Fountain of Life Covenant Church, Madison, Wisconsin

THE POWER

OF THE

72

ORDINARY DISCIPLES IN
EXTRAORDINARY EVANGELISM

JOHN TETER

IVP Books

An imprint of InterVarsity Press
Downers Grove, Illinois

InterVarsity Press
P.O. Box 1400, Downers Grove, IL 60515-1426
ivpress.com
email@ivpress.com

InterVarsity Press® is the book-publishing division of InterVarsity Christian Fellowship/USA®, a movement of students and faculty active on campus at hundreds of universities, colleges, and schools of nursing in the United States of America, and a member movement of the International Fellowship of Evangelical Students. For information about local and regional activities, visit intervarsity.org.

Cover design: David Fassett
Interior design: Daniel van Loon
Images: grey background: © GOLDsquirrel/iStockphoto
skyline of Chicago: © marchello74/iStockphoto

ISBN 978-0-8308-4517-0 (print)
ISBN 978-0-8308-8899-3 (digital)

Printed in the United States of America ♾

InterVarsity Press is committed to ecological stewardship and to the conservation of natural resources in all our operations. This book was printed using sustainably sourced paper.

Library of Congress Cataloging-in-Publication Data
A catalog record for this book is available from the Library of Congress.

P	21	20	19	18	17	16	15	14	13	12	11	10	9	8	7	6	5	4	3	2	1
Y	34	33	32	31	30	29	28	27	26	25	24	23	22	21	20	19	18	17			

For Joy, Kara, and Luke

May you follow Jesus closely
and with your very own eyes
see Satan fall like lightning from heaven

CONTENTS

Foreword by Darrell Johnson   1

Introduction: Welcome to the Power of the 72   3

PART 1: THEOLOGY

1 Faith Comes First   21

2 Sent to the Poor   37

3 Wolves, Bears, and Crushing Pressure   55

PART 2: APPLICATION

4 How People Become Christians   71

5 Earnest and Powerful Prayers   89

6 Friends: Secular to Sacred   109

7 Experience: Healing and Hearing   127

8 Conversion: Rejoice with Me   143

Epilogue: A Final Benediction   153

Acknowledgments   155

Notes   159

After this the Lord appointed seventy-two others and sent them on ahead of him, two by two, into every town and place where he himself was about to go. And he said to them, "The harvest is plentiful, but the laborers are few. Therefore pray earnestly to the Lord of the harvest to send out laborers into his harvest. Go your way; behold, I am sending you out as lambs in the midst of wolves. Carry no moneybag, no knapsack, no sandals, and greet no one on the road. Whatever house you enter, first say, 'Peace be to this house!' And if a son of peace is there, your peace will rest upon him. But if not, it will return to you. And remain in the same house, eating and drinking what they provide, for the laborer deserves his wages. Do not go from house to house. Whenever you enter a town and they receive you, eat what is set before you. Heal the sick in it and say to them, 'The kingdom of God has come near to you.' But whenever you enter a town and they do not receive you, go into its streets and say, 'Even the dust of your town that clings to our feet we wipe off against you. Nevertheless know this, that the kingdom of God has come near.' I tell you, it will be more bearable on that day for Sodom than for that town.

"Woe to you, Chorazin! Woe to you, Bethsaida! For if the mighty works done in you had been done in Tyre and Sidon, they would have repented long ago, sitting in sackcloth and ashes. But it will be more bearable in the judgment for Tyre and Sidon than for you. And you, Capernaum, will you be exalted to heaven? You shall be brought down to Hades.

"The one who hears you hears me, and the one who rejects you rejects me, and the one who rejects me rejects him who sent me."

The seventy-two returned with joy, saying, "Lord, even the demons are subject to us in your name!" And he said to them, "I saw Satan fall like lightning from heaven. Behold, I have given you authority to tread on serpents and scorpions, and over all the power of the enemy, and nothing shall hurt you. Nevertheless, do not rejoice in this, that the spirits are subject to you, but rejoice that your names are written in heaven."

LUKE 10:1-20

FOREWORD

Darrell Johnson

John Teter is exactly the right person to write a book on ordinary disciples engaged in extraordinary evangelism. John is an extraordinary ordinary disciple of Jesus, the extraordinary Evangelist. From the day he surrendered to Jesus' call upon his life, John has manifested—and lived—the spiritual gift of evangelism. He "oozes" the winsome joy, contagious enthusiasm, compassionate courage, and unquenchable energy of one captured by he who is life itself. I have known John for decades now, and I walk away from every encounter with him saying, "Lord, I wish I could be more like him."

In his now-classic work *The Master Plan of Evangelism*, Robert E. Coleman identifies the qualities Jesus seeks in those he calls to join him in winning the world into his kingdom. "None of them occupied prominent places in the Synagogue, nor did any of them belong to the Levitical priesthood. For the most part they were common laboring men [and women], probably having no professional training beyond the rudiments of knowledge necessary for their vocations."[1] They were not wealthy, except perhaps the sons

---

[1] Robert E. Coleman, *The Master Plan of Evangelism* (Los Angeles: Rusthoi, 1963).

of Zebedee, who ran a thriving fishing business. None had degrees from academic institutions. "One might wonder how Jesus could ever use them." Yet Jesus chose them because, argues Coleman, "they were teachable." They had big hearts, and they yearned for God and the reality of his life and kingdom. They were "pliable in the hands of the Master."

Coleman is describing John Teter! Teachable, pliable, yearning for all that Jesus has and wants to give us. I stand amazed at just how much Jesus has taught my brother.

So read the journey of how Jesus has used his teachable disciple to build a thriving ministry among ordinary disciples in the heart of the city. Follow John into the world of Luke 10, where Jesus sends seventy-two "wonder how Jesus could ever use them" ordinary people into the world with his good news. And you will, like me, find yourself invigorated by the life-giving dynamism of extraordinary evangelism.

Thank you, John, for being so teachable, and for teaching me what an authentic disciple looks like in our world.

WELCOME TO THE POWER OF THE 72

You know what to do. We have trained you.
Let's play Orioles baseball.

COACH EDGAR ORTIZ

THE WEST LONG BEACH ORIOLES

Little League baseball has been one of our family's great joys in recent years. My wife, Becky, and I have a seven-year-old daughter, Kara, who from birth has lived her life with great energy, passion, and focus. And she has always loved sports. When she was in tee-ball, we played against the Tigers, coached by Edgar Ortiz. At age five, Kara pointed out how good the Tigers were, and she even prayed at bedtime that Edgar would someday be her coach. Through a series of circumstances, her prayers were answered, and I became Edgar's assistant coach on the Farm Ball Orioles.

Edgar grew up in West Long Beach, played baseball for Compton College, was drafted by the Detroit Tigers, and made it all the way to minor league AA before an injury ended his playing career. A giant man with an even bigger heart for children, his unique blend of stature, experience, and communication style make him one of the best coaches around. He is passionate about teaching kids the technical aspects of the game of baseball, while making sure he can see their teeth—because they're smiling.

At the early practices, Edgar taught the Orioles to hold the ball correctly and then taught them how to step and turn their shoulders. Next he focused on release points and aiming the throw at a teammate's chest. They learned how to throw, catch, and field ground balls. They learned how to hit and run the bases. Soon the concentration on details paid great dividends, and each of the kids improved. Our team came together in a way we never hoped or imagined.

The 2016 Orioles season was magical. We went 24-1, won our Silverado Park league, and then went on to defeat six other leagues to win the Southern California District 38 Tournament of Champions. The Orioles were neither the biggest kids nor the most talented, but they played with great heart and sound fundamentals. When the pressure was on, our children were able to execute the technical skills of the game.

Kara played first base for the Orioles, and the coaches recognized her contributions by voting her onto the all-star team. Coach Edgar left the meeting after the vote and came directly to our house to tell her the good news. She was asleep, but we woke her up so Edgar could tell her in person. I will never forget the joy on her face; she immediately wrapped her arms around Edgar's neck, covering his Dallas Cowboys tattoo with her little arms. He hugged her and said, "I'm proud of you, mama."

I learned an important lesson serving on Edgar's coaching staff. To execute, players needed technical training, not just head knowledge. Very few players could explain the strategy or nuances of the game. While six- and seven-year-old minds sometimes focused on the dirt or picking the daisy in front of them, their bodies still knew how to throw, catch, and hit when the pressure was on. Every year on opening day, Silverado Park will raise the 2016 Farm Ball Orioles championship banner because Edgar and our coaching staff taught the kids to play Orioles baseball.

Just as young players must learn fundamentals to help them execute during games, so disciples must learn practical skills to become effective evangelists. Luke's Gospel provides a remarkable account of how Jesus called seventy-two disciples, taught them how to be evangelists, and watched them accomplish great things for God's kingdom. If six- and seven-year-olds can listen to their coach to win a baseball championship, how much more can we learn from our Master when eternal joy or punishment hang in the balance for every human soul.

I'M ONE OF THE 72

To provide some perspective and context, allow me to introduce myself. I'm the son of a Dutch-American father and a Korean mother. My parents met on a steamship on a journey from Seattle to Seoul in 1958. My mother was returning to Korea to tell her family that she had secured her dream job in Los Angeles. My father was a mariner on the ship. They fell in love during the three-week trip across the Pacific Ocean. Their long voyage certainly puts international travel today in perspective.

I was born and raised in Los Angeles and currently live in Long Beach with my amazing wife and our three wonderful children, Joy, Kara, and Luke. I didn't grow up in a Christian home; I came to faith through InterVarsity Christian Fellowship at the University of California, Los Angeles, when I was twenty-two.

After I had served for twelve years with InterVarsity, the Holy Spirit called us to plant a church in our inner-city neighborhood of West Long Beach. Becky and I like to joke that Fountain of Life Covenant Church (FOL) is our fourth child. Since our home base is the local church, many of the illustrations and stories in this book come from FOL. It's our testimony that as we have gone out as a pair, we have seen "Satan fall like lightning from heaven" (Luke 10:18). God has given power to our feeble attempts to heal the city and declare the kingdom of God to bring many to faith. We hope to pass along the lessons, both good and bad, to inspire you to experience God's power in evangelism for yourself.

Pastor Charles Simeon is one of my Christian heroes. He ministered at the same church in Cambridge, England, for fifty-four years. For much of that time, he served as a working pastor, leading his church and participating in national and international missions. Following the Simeon model, I have served as a pastor and simultaneously served with the Evangelical Covenant Church and Fountain of Life Antioch, our local effort to help plant new churches from Jackson, Mississippi, and Marion, Indiana, to Hong Kong. I'm grateful for what God is teaching me as I serve and learn in local, national, and international ministry circles and as I seek to be a faithful witness for Jesus "in Jerusalem and in all Judea and Samaria, and to the end of the earth" (Acts 1:8).

I love to share my faith. It brings me so much joy to be a small part of another person coming to faith. I believe God has given me the spiritual gift of evangelism, so I try to use that gift in my personal friendships and public preaching. The call for evangelism draws me deeply into texts like Luke 10, and I'm proud to call myself "one of the 72."

CORE BOOK STUDY AND LUKE'S GOSPEL

Christian leadership is hard, but frontline evangelism with people who reject you is even harder. As God calls us to challenging ministry, he equips us to meet the tests and trials we'll experience. In my experience, mastering core books of the Bible has given me strength and ministry insights. Core-book Bible study involves in-depth study of contexts and historical backgrounds, including the analysis of verses, chapters, and sections. The author of the book becomes a mentor and, in some mystical manner, a friend. Because of the large amount of time I have spent in Luke through Acts, I like to say that Luke has become my homie.

Living in Luke's Gospel has framed my church-planting experience. We chose our home and our context for ministry because of Jesus' mission statement in Luke 4. Our church has a one-verse vision that comes from Luke 10:2: we are kingdom workers. Our evangelism model is based on the sending of the 72. It is my testimony that as I attempted to master Luke's Gospel, Luke's Gospel mastered me. It took me almost two years to complete the twenty-four chapters, and I've learned many concepts from studying and applying Luke's Gospel to my life and ministry.

For the reader's convenience, each chapter in *The Power of 72* contains an insert stating the chapter theme and core text.

CHAPTER THEME: Live today as one of the 72.

CORE TEXT: Overview of Luke 10:1-2

> After this the Lord appointed seventy-two others and sent them on ahead of him, two by two, into every town and place where he himself was about to go. And he said to them, "The harvest is plentiful, but the laborers are few. Therefore pray earnestly to the Lord of the harvest to send out laborers into his harvest."

ANONYMOUS EVANGELISTS

This chapter is an invitation to become part of God's good work of reaching the world.

A wise preaching mentor once told me, "Live in the text until the text lives in you." I pray that these same words will be your experience as we journey together in the good news of Luke 10. It begins with a detailed account of the training and ministry experience of seventy-two anonymous evangelists and ends with one of Jesus' most famous stories, the parable of the good Samaritan.

When I became the director of church planting for the Evangelical Covenant Church, I asked God to give our team a vision that was grounded in his Word, which is timeless and inspirational. I remember where I was standing when God's Spirit led us to Luke 10:1-24. It felt as though the Lord had indeed spoken to our hearts and minds. I love the biblical model of anonymous but faithful disciples who engage their world with the news—not the advice—of the gospel. Not only does the world need this vision, but as disciples of Jesus, *we* need it.

We know very little about the 72, and I think this was Luke's intention. Because we have a number, some believe that this number is symbolic. For example, scholars have argued that seventy-two refers to the number of apostles (twelve) times the number that symbolizes man (six). The number twelve highlights the strength, power, and vision of God. The six shines light on man: created on the sixth day, sinner, unable to change the human heart.

Another reading is that seventy-two was the number of known countries in the world during Jesus' time. The Lord of the harvest was symbolically sending out an evangelist for each country. This theory highlights God's heart for all countries, especially the Gentile ones.

I believe Luke introduces the evangelists this way so we see ourselves in the story. It's no accident that we don't know their names, genders, ages, or spiritual gifts. We also don't know their personality profiles. Their anonymity allows us to pause and wonder if we could be among the seventy-two disciples. It might be hard to picture ourselves planting churches all over the ancient world like Paul, preaching a fiery first sermon before a hostile crowd of three thousand people, or like Priscilla mentoring Apollos (Acts 18:26). We know their names because they are the all-stars. But the 72 were unknown rookies just like you and me.

We have very little data about them. One could argue that the only certainty we have is that Jesus hand-selected them to deliver the message of salvation. The living God personally called them, trained them, and sent them to be a part of his evangelism team.

There are so many great moments in the first four Gospels. I often wish I could have been a fly on the wall, watching Jesus and his leadership team in action. If it were possible to travel back in time, the evangelism training seminar from Luke 10 would be at the top of my list. What led up to the 72 arriving for their briefing? Imagine receiving an email, phone call, or text from Jesus of Nazareth, inviting you to be a part of his new ministry team. What grace would have been conveyed if you were under the personal training of the Lord Jesus himself!

Jesus called, trained, and sent these followers into an unknown and strategic mission field. The 72 were the answer to his earnest prayers to the Lord of the harvest. And they were found faithful in accomplishing the mission God had set before them. Although they were like lambs among wolves, joy awaited them at the finish line.

But let's be honest. They must have been terrified.

Have you ever jumped off a high dive into a swimming pool? The clear blue water seems a hundred miles beneath your feet, and fear arises as you look behind you and see others urging you to jump. I remember that terrifying moment vividly. In high school, I worked at a tennis center that had an Olympic-size pool with a ten-meter diving board. My lifeguard friends always warned us, "Don't look down, or your face will suffer the consequences." When it was your turn to jump from the high dive, there was no turning back.

I imagine that the seventy-two disciples felt a similar fear on the morning when Jesus sent them out. He sent seventy-two people into a hostile environment. And he addressed the inner workings of their hearts and their fears when he said his missionaries would be like sheep among wolves.

Yet, despite this fearsome image, they returned with joy. All of them.

It would have been enough for thirty-six to return with joy and incredible if sixty-four returned with joy, but the text clearly states that all seventy-two returned with joy (Luke 24:52). This teaches us that we can actually accomplish the mission. In some mysterious way, the work of God through these seventy-two caused movement in the spiritual realm.

The lives of the 72 teach us that evangelism is not just for the spiritually gifted. The good and hard work of evangelism is a call for all disciples at all times.

THE POWER OF THE 72

The title of this book includes the word *power*. The 72, our rookie evangelists, wouldn't have considered themselves to be in positions of power. A lamb does not have the place of power when wolves are present. The Lord had to train them how to deal with their emotions, their fears, and the rejection they would face. Yet their ministry had a massive impact in the spiritual realm.

The Lord "saw Satan fall like lightning from heaven" (Luke 10:18). I think this means that in the next dimension, which only God, angels, and the spiritual beings can see, the devil lost significant positional authority. The work of the 72 didn't cause

Satan to fall physically from another dimension into the South China Sea. No, their work caused a shift in the eternal realm that brought the devil and his dark kingdom crashing down. These are the kind of results one might expect from disciples named Paul, John, and Peter.

Three Greek words used in the New Testament are translated as *power* in English. The first is *dynamis*, the explosive nature of power, from which we get the word *dynamite*. The second word for power is *energeia*, from which *energy* is derived. The third word is *kratos* (the root for "-cracy"), which denotes authority. I believe that as Jesus called, trained, and sent the 72, all three words were in play.

The 72 were sent to demonstrate the same explosive power of God that raised Jesus from the dead. Prayers, healing, and miraculous signs validated their message. They were sent with great energy and zeal to love, serve, and bring new life to the city. They were sent with the authority of the emperor of the universe and were so aligned with his authority and the knowledge that if they were rejected, it was God himself who was rejected. That's a massive amount of power that can't be seen by the human eye.

Pastor and author Darrell Johnson reminds us that our mission always flows from our relationship with Jesus. The transference of his authority onto the 72 only strengthens this idea. Johnson wrote, "You can see that the three great disciplines of discipleship— worship, community, mission—cannot be separated because they are grounded in the Trinity. Co-lovers with God is worship. Co-lovers with God of one another is community. Co-lovers with God of the world is mission."[1]

A last dimension of power is the 72 operating as a team. Standing alone, the newly appointed evangelists would have had a difficult time embracing and overcoming the challenges. But there was a power to draw from as they were together. Each evangelist was given an immediate partner. Each two-person ministry team was part of a much bigger thirty-six-person evangelism battalion. Together, there were seventy-two personalities, seventy-two diverse perspectives, seventy-two prayers, and seventy-two voices.

These anonymous evangelists were sent in God's explosive, forceful, and ruling power. This was power beyond measure. This was power that never burns out. This was power that is never thwarted. Alone there would have been little power. But in Jesus and on mission together, the 72 were powerful enough to unseat Satan himself and throw him down to earth.

ONE

In *Zero to One*, Peter Thiel, the creator of PayPal, argued that the most significant development in the life of a company is not moving from a hundred to a thousand to one hundred thousand to one million. The most important step of growth is creating something new and moving the needle from zero to one. He wrote, "Indeed, the single most powerful pattern I have noticed is that successful people find value in unexpected places, and they do this by thinking about people first instead of formulas."[2]

When we move from zero to one, we create a template of sorts and a baseline for learning. I wonder if when Jesus trained the 72 for evangelism, he had the number one in mind. Luke 15, often called "the gospel within the third gospel," is full of that number. There is one lost sheep, one lost coin, one immoral son, and one lost religious son. And the shepherd, the woman, and the father all do everything they can to find that lost one.

I believe in goals. Pushing yourself beyond your comfort zone to complete a project at work, achieve a higher score on an exam, or win a tough tennis match takes a goal as well as a commitment to reach that goal. As you work through the chapters ahead, consider setting the number one as your goal. If you're able to move your evangelism ministry from zero to one, you will have learned to live as one of the 72.

Let me provide an example of getting from zero to one. I met Robert during the first year of our church plant. When planting a new church, a pastor must be open, available, and aware of how God might be leading. Following Paul's model in Acts 16, I wanted to make sure I was a part of the daily rhythms of public life. It's nearly impossible to plant a church from behind a desk, so I regularly prayed, studied, sent emails, and met with people at our local Starbucks.

Rob was doing some class work at a table next to me. He was a biracial twenty-three-year-old student at Cal State Long Beach, majoring in accounting. We quickly bonded over being biracial and our mutual love of sports: lots and lots of sports. Since FOL was hosting an outreach basketball tournament, I invited Rob.

A few days later, I saw him again, this time at another Starbucks. I told him I was a pastor and that I wanted to show how much God cared about him by buying him a specialty drink. He shared a bit about his faith background and how he hadn't been to church in years, but that he was very open. We exchanged numbers, and he shared again how excited he was for the big hoops tournament.

The tournament came, and Rob didn't show up. I was surprised that he missed it, so I called him to check up and let him know I was thinking about him. He picked up the phone and apologized for not being able to play, especially because he always tried to keep his word. I told him it wasn't that big a deal. I then heard what sounded like machines beeping in the background again and again. I began to put the pieces together, and I asked, "Are you in the hospital?"

"Yeah, man. I'm in the hospital."

"Are you okay, bro?" I asked.

"I'm not doing too hot," he answered.

"What happened, Rob?"

"I was down at the shoreline last night with my buddies. We ran into some rough dudes, and a fight broke out. I jumped in to try and help my homie a little bit. And I got shot three times."

So I visited Rob at the hospital. When I asked about his family, he told me his mother died when he was five, and his father was never around after the death. Having lost my own father to a plane accident when I was a boy, I understood something about his loss, pain, and the challenges of growing up without a parent. I prayed for Rob, lifting him up to Jesus, who works all things for good.

Rob's Christian conversion became one of my first templates for how young people in the city come to faith. Ten years later, Rob and I are thankful for how God brought us into friendship. Today he is a committed disciple of Jesus, deepening and growing as one of the 72. We laugh together about the best excuse ever for not coming to a basketball tournament.

The woman pursued and found one lost coin. The church planter pursued and found one lost college student.

My hope and prayer is that this book will (1) provide a clear theological foundation for evangelism and the call to first preach the gospel to the poor; (2) present my theory of process conversion, which has been field-tested in America and Asia for close to five years, so that you know how non-Christians come to faith; (3) call you to master four ministry tasks that are central to personal evangelism; and (4) prepare you for daily rejection by providing the perspective of eternal joy.

STRUCTURE AND FEATURES

The Power of the 72 has two parts. Following a very loose model based on Paul's letters, the first half of the book is theology. The second half is application. I'm a firm believer that Christian ministry needs a strong balance of orthodoxy (what we believe) and orthopraxy (what we do).

Part one explains the theology of ministry flowing out of being, evangelism that prioritizes the poor, and a fresh understanding of persecution and suffering. It's my desire to teach the Scripture with hermeneutic integrity and appropriate intensity.

Part two provides practical input on how to "do" evangelism with real people. Chapter four, "How People Become Christians," defines process conversion and introduces a timeline that has three features: four benchmark events; three conversion conversations we must initiate with our friends; and two ministry tools. My research has identified the benchmark events present in process conversion: (1) trusting a non-Christian; (2) experiencing God and the good news of the gospel; (3) hearing and understanding the good news; and (4) receiving a clear call to follow Jesus.

To help our non-Christian friends progress through the benchmarks, they need three conversations. "Conversion Conversation 1: Initial Investigation" shows how small talk breaks the ice and makes a connection. If you're already friends with non-Christians, you've completed this first conversation. "Conversion Conversation 2: Secular to Sacred" is a personal invitation for our friends to study the Bible for themselves. "Conversion Conversation 3: From Curiosity to the Cross" is a clear call to biblical faith. Each ministry task builds on itself toward leading our friends to faith in Jesus. I will pass along my experiences and understanding through "Habits of the 72." I'll also share real-life examples from my own life and ministry as well as from FOL lay leaders.

The illustrations recorded in this book include both positive and not-so-positive evangelism interactions. More than ever, we need to be thoughtful in our communication style and word choices. If any of these illustrations encourage you, that brings joy to my heart. I write as a broken sinner keenly aware of my depraved and sinful nature. I tell many of my own stories because I know them best, and I hope that I don't come across as proud or self-promoting. I believe with all my heart that ministry is truly a gift from God.

My personal philosophy is that an evangelism book is fundamentally informative and inspirational. The genre and format limit implementation concepts. For more technical training resources, please visit folantioch.org.

PRAYER OF COMMITMENT

I believe that you're reading this book because God is calling you to live as one of the 72. But you're likely in need of both training and power. The second half of the book will help you pray and develop spiritual friendships, help your friends experience God's healing, and help you call them to faith. Above all else, may you rejoice that your name is written in heaven.

Please take a moment to ask God to empower you and train you to do today just what he trained his first evangelism team to do. I pray that you have many experiences that you know are designed by God himself. And may you have many of your own stories of courageous evangelism to treasure in your heart and share with your friends and family.

In the Gospels, ministry success is not based on how many people come to an event. Jesus had five thousand come to a preview service, but did they leave with faith and share the news? Coming to an event that provides some free bread and healing requires no personal sacrifice. Ministry success is not based on how many come, but on how many go. Being sent as an evangelist requires faith. You can't fake healing the city and preaching the gospel. In the kingdom math, 72 > 5,000.

I am one of the 72. You are one of the 72. Together, may the Spirit call us, train us, and send us to our non-Christian friends. They need us so much more than we can ever think or imagine.

Joy and rejection await.

PART

1

THEOLOGY

FAITH COMES FIRST

The first great and primary business
to which I ought to attend every day is to
have my soul happy in the Lord.

GEORGE MUELLER

IF I HAD A TATTOO

I do not have a tattoo. I have always been afraid of needles, and I hear that tattoos are addictive. Yet there are many interesting tattoos in our church, especially among the younger people. I was particularly moved when Tamika had the number 72 tattooed on the inside of her right wrist after we preached through Luke 10. I joked with her that she would never forget that sermon series.

I've often wondered what verse of Scripture I would get tattooed on my body, if I ever found enough courage to venture down that road. The answer is easy: Ezekiel 16:6-8.

During my first year as a disciple of Jesus, I committed to pray one hour a day. I wanted to give God my best. I found a place to pray, made it my own, and went there every single day to pray for one hour. My daily prayer time became a very life-giving habit, and it rewards me to this day.

Part of my prayer time includes listening. In a healthy and vibrant relationship, both people talk to one another. I didn't want to be the child who only talks and asks but never listens to my Father. I had been following Jesus hard for nine months, and I had met God in my personal devotions. The Spirit convicted me as I read the Word and listened to sermons. I was clearly growing, but I had never heard "the still small voice" of God, like Elijah in 1 Kings 19:12.

I had a few friends who were more mature in the faith, and they told me stories about "what God told me" or "what God said to me." It blew my mind that they had heard the good Shepherd's voice. I desperately wanted to hear his voice, so I gave him an entire year of faithful devotion.

On May 16, 1993, I finally heard God speak to me. That morning, I asked him a question, and then I listened. I was like Jacob, ready to wrestle with God so I would be blessed with his voice. My question was "God, how much do you love me?" Immediately, I heard in my soul the beautiful voice of the Shepherd say, "John, read Ezekiel 16:6-8."

At that point in my discipleship, I was unaware of the Old Testament prophets. If you had asked me who Ezekiel was, I might have said the running back for the Dallas Cowboys. I thumbed through the Bible, hoping that the book existed. I was encouraged when I found that Ezekiel was, in fact, a book in the Bible. Did it have sixteen chapters? Yes. It actually had forty-eight.

I read Ezekiel 16:6-8 with tears forming in my eyes. My heart skipped a beat, and I wanted to take off my shoes, because I knew I was on holy ground. For the first time, I was having an adult conversation with the Father.

When I was a boy, I lost my father to a glider plane accident. The trauma and pain of that loss launched me into a dangerous pattern of isolation, self-medication, and reckless living. Rich and meaningful long-term relationships were rare for me. As a boy, I probably would have been diagnosed with abandonment disorder, but counseling was rare, and even if we wanted it, we didn't have money to invest in something like that. Because of my loss, I kept most of my friends and family at a distance. I protected myself from loving too deeply, because people in this world could go up in the air to fly and never come back down. I remember hating the fact that this life is temporary. I had next to no control over anything, and I was aware that the greatest people in life could be taken away without notice.

As a new baby in the faith, I never considered how the accident and loss of my dad affected my relationship with God. I'm sure I projected much of my pain onto God, and at some level I blamed him. Still, I wanted the stability, the longevity, and the unchanging love that I thought he offered. If Jesus really was offering me a way to get off this miserable planet rotating in space and to land in a place that was secure, safe, and eternal, I wanted that with all my heart.

This was good news, but it seemed too good to be true. I had always imagined God to be a cold-hearted judge waiting to sentence me in his courtroom. Deep down, I hoped God would be the Father I always needed.

A parable about God's relationship with Israel, Ezekiel 16:6-8 describes how circumstances led Israel to suffer the terrifying shame of being a baby abandoned and left to die in a field. In the parable, the baby squirms in its own blood, writhing and struggling for life. I quickly identified with that image, because even as I tried to keep everything under control, my internal pain increased with each passing year.

God passes by the field and says to the baby, "Live!" He takes the baby home, cares for it, and gives it the very best things in life. He watches the baby grow up and become a beautiful adult. When the baby is old enough, God enters into an everlasting covenant and marries the baby who was once left to die in the field. The passage ends with a declaration: "I made my vow to you and entered into a covenant with you . . . and you became mine" (v. 8). As someone who worried that those closest to me would be taken away, this was the best news I had ever heard. Tears began to fall on my Bible.

As I read God's words to me, my soul caught fire. The image of the baby in the field captured my loneliness, my insecurity, my fear, and my anger about how life had done me wrong. It put to words the overwhelming feelings of vulnerability. From that moment, I knew I wanted God; I wanted to live with him and experience all he had for me. I wanted him to give me a new life.

That day I felt God make a massive deposit to fill the cavernous hole in my soul. Even now, the boyhood pain, fear, and anger still exist, but God has brought peace to the raging waves of my soul. He has given me a wonderful family that loves me and walks with me through my struggles, and he has given me hope about that day when I will begin to experience the everlasting covenant from the other side of eternity. The God who speaks Ezekiel 16:6-8 is my only hope and my portion forever. My faith is anchored in the living God being a father to the fatherless.

CHAPTER THEME: Evangelism flows from our relationship with God.

CORE TEXT: Overview of Luke 10:17-22

> *The seventy-two returned with joy, saying, "Lord, even the demons are subject to us in your name!" And he said to them, "I saw Satan fall like lightning from heaven. Behold, I have given you authority to tread on serpents and scorpions, and over all the power of the enemy, and nothing shall hurt you. Nevertheless, do not rejoice in this, that the spirits are subject to you, but rejoice that your names are written in heaven."*

In that same hour he rejoiced in the Holy Spirit and said, "I thank you, Father, Lord of heaven and earth, that you have hidden these things from the wise and understanding and revealed them to little children; yes, Father, for such was your gracious will. All things have been handed over to me by my Father, and no one knows who the Son is except the Father, or who the Father is except the Son and anyone to whom the Son chooses to reveal him."

DO NOT REJOICE IN CIRCUMSTANCES

Luke 10:17-19 describes an amazing moment, the triumphant return of thirty-six ministry teams. Like a sports team that has just won a championship, their locker room, covered in tarps to keep valuables dry, is filled with reporters and news cameras prepared for jubilant interviews. Players run in, grab their championship gear, goggles, and bottles of champagne, and prepare to celebrate.

The 72 completed their task, and it was time for the party to begin. They not only rejoiced in what they'd accomplished, but they likely breathed a collective sigh of relief after finishing such a hard ministry task.

Jesus trained the 72 for personal evangelism. He introduced the concept of opposition and persecution, and he taught them how to respond to unbelieving and potentially hostile people. At the evangelism training day, however, the name Satan didn't appear in the training manual. Nonetheless, in some mysterious way, the efforts of seventy-two faithful evangelists put a dent in the strategic plans of the one who deceived Adam and Eve in the garden.

Imagine their joy as they shared about their power—and authority—over the devil. These mere human beings had received Jesus' *kratos* (authoritative power) over the devil and his demonic host. In the name of Jesus, they were able to cast demons out of men, women, and children. When the 72 spoke, the dark spirits that Paul called the principalities and authorities were expelled from their demonic posts (see Ephesians 6:12). How could our friends not be full of joy? How could they not jump up and down? And yet Jesus corrected them at that amazing moment.

It wasn't wrong for them to rejoice. The Lord didn't rebuke them or command them to stop celebrating. He offered pastoral admonishment because they were rejoicing in the wrong thing. Ministry results can be very fickle, and Jesus doesn't want us to base our joy on things that can be taken away. He encouraged the 72 to find joy in something far more permanent. Would they always have authority over the demons? Would every evangelistic mission trip result in Satan falling like lightning from heaven? Jesus directed them to a much better celebration with even greater returns of joy.

Today's disciple must understand that evangelism doesn't secure favor with God. We don't earn God's love; we share God's love. At the very moment when the 72 wanted to high-five one another for all they'd done for God, Jesus stopped them to remind them that they had already won the spiritual lottery. True evangelism always moves *from* the victory, never *toward* the victory.

REJOICE IN RELATIONSHIP

Luke 10:20-22 is one of three times in the book when the author identifies the entire Trinity by name. God the Father, God the Son, and God the Holy Spirit have significant roles in the plan for Mary to birth Jesus (Luke 1:35-37). God the Father sends God the Son and anoints him with God the Holy Spirit in his first sermon (Luke 4:16-21). The presence of the Trinity in these three sections displays Luke's emphasis on the subject of each passage. Father, Son, and Spirit each play a role in the incarnation, the mission to the margins, and the salvation of sinners.

Jesus loves his witnesses and wants us to understand that our joy should be rooted in who we are, not what we do. The fact that we engage in incredibly successful mission is far less important than being born of God in Jesus' celebration rankings. Jesus commanded the 72 to rejoice that God had written their names in heaven. This supreme blessing of assurance surpasses the fluctuating results of ministry, especially when we stop to consider that without God's prompting, pursuit, and unending patience, we wouldn't have faith or relationship with him.

One of the great American missionaries, David Brainerd, wrote in his journal what it means that Jesus has written his name in heaven: "Oh, if I ever get to heaven it will be because God wills, and nothing else; for I never did anything of myself but get away from God! My soul will be astonished at the unsearchable riches of divine grace when I arrive at the mansions."[1]

The prayer recorded in Luke 10:20-21 is of supreme theological importance because it captures the Son of God's understanding of Christian conversion. This is Luke's condensed version of Jesus' high-priestly prayer in John 17. The reader understands that God is absolutely sovereign and chooses to whom he will reveal the kingdom of God. The divine mysteries stay hidden from the wise as God graciously chooses to reveal them to the babes.

Jesus' prayer closely parallels Mary's Spirit-filled song (Luke 1:46-55). Both she and her Son are full of joy (v. 47). Both Mary and her Son speak of God's mercy and his might (v. 52). Both Mary and her Son reveal God's purposes to lift the low and the babes, while bringing down the proud and wise of the world (vv. 51-53). Both prayers reinforce the social upheaval that Jesus' kingdom causes in the world. Mary and Jesus of Nazareth rejoice in the wisdom of God to bring into his family those that are low, vulnerable, and needy, while sovereignly choosing to hide it from those who enjoy privilege and status in the world.

Because Jesus turns the world upside down, the true way up is actually down.

FAITH IN LUKE'S GOSPEL

The 72 were ordinary men and women—and maybe even children—who followed Jesus. These normal people heard Jesus teach in public and private settings, and like the disciples on the Emmaus road in Luke 24, their hearts burned within them when they heard his words. Or perhaps they experienced a display of God's power, which not only authenticated the message of good news but also declared Jesus' spiritual authority. While we don't know the details of their conversions, it's important for us to remember that these evangelists were the first converts.

To be one of the 72 is to be a person who has experienced the goodness of God and embraced his call of discipleship. The 72 were likely present when Jesus unveiled the "Constitution of the Kingdom" (Luke 6:20-46). Having named new leadership for God's community, he then defined the expectations of devoted followers who were filled with the Holy Spirit. I believe the 72 were chosen because they were already people of faith. They weren't selected because of their giftedness and future potential; they were selected because they loved Jesus and his coming kingdom.

The Luke 6 Constitution still applies to us today. If we are part of the 72, we are to be content with our poverty, because the kingdom of God belongs to the poor (v. 20). We are called to avoid riches, so we don't receive our consolation on earth (v. 24). We live by faith by loving our enemies and blessing those who curse us (v. 27). The 72 follow the merciful God by loving freely those who can't pay us back, doing more than the sinners in our world (vv. 34-35).

The call to mission doesn't increase our favor or status with God. If we are in the faith, God has revealed to us what he has hidden from the kings of the world. We can't improve upon being a child of God. Mission, therefore, enhances and deepens our faith relationship with Jesus. The mission of God drives us deeper, further, and higher into the person of God. The community of Israel became God's people when he called them to himself and gave them commands to protect and enhance their relationship (Exodus 20:1-17). The commands of God are never meant to be a burden. In fact, they offer protection, security, and an invitation to intimacy. New Testament scholar Joel Green sheds great light on their discipleship mindset: "His is a message of total transformation, with a consistency of goodness between the inside and outside of a person. Hearing is never enough."[2]

Jesus calls sinners to become new believers in his community. Members of his family are called to obey in faith. He didn't call seventy-two random people to execute an outreach mission. He called disciples who knew and loved him. Faith always comes first before mission.

On a leadership note, I've noticed that some people begin living the path of the 72, only to stop running the race. What causes them to stop is not a lack of technical skills, theological training, or cultural insights. Dr. J. Robert Clinton, the pioneer of Leadership Emergence Theory, wrote, "Repeated anecdotal evidence from modern day leadership indicates that numerous leaders are failing in ministry. The phrase, 'Few leaders finish well' provides a chilling warning to leaders such as you and me, and indeed to all of us who want to finish well."[3]

I believe the problem of finishing well boils down to a faith that crumbles under the pressure of team dynamics, persecution, temptation, and discouraging results in challenging mission contexts. To put it plainly, our faith runs out. Our love for Jesus grows cold. Many promising young Christians are promoted to positions of leadership too early and never recover their first love for God.

Many Christians do not have the primary goal of having their souls happy in God. In Revelation, Jesus exhorted the church in

Ephesus, the most impressive and fruitful church in all of Asia Minor, to return to their first love (Revelation 2:1-7). Pastor Darrell Johnson helps us understand this concept: "What is first love? First love is the love experienced by two people who are 'in love.' First love is the love we had for Jesus when he first broke through to us and won us by his love. Jesus says that for all of their hard work, patient endurance, and orthodoxy, the Ephesians were no longer 'in love' with him. Affection and intimacy were gone."[4]

They were so busy with meetings, training conferences, and leading the growing church that they forgot about Jesus. Where love once reigned and brought great joy, success snuck in and stole the life. I wonder how many Christian leaders today still have the very things that won them to Christ active in their lives. We must make faithfully living out the deeds of our first love our highest priority; yet it's so hard to keep our first love. Many of us resonate with the words of Peter Scazzero as he described his transition from new Christian to a leader in God's kingdom: "When I first became a Christian, I fell in love with Jesus. I cherished time alone with him while reading the Bible and praying. But it wasn't long before I was engaged in more activity for God than my being with God could sustain."[5]

As we move ahead, I hope you will consider your experience of falling in love with Jesus. Do you cherish and protect times of prayer, Bible study, and intimate worship? Jesus, rejoicing in the Holy Spirit, can't contain his delight in God initiating with us while we were far outside his kingdom. There is great spiritual power and life to be accessed in the foundations of our faith.

HAPPY IN THE LORD

I began following Jesus on May 8, 1992. Since then, with varying degrees of success, I've made it my first priority to know and love the living God. From my first days of following Jesus, I knew I needed to know God. I had a growing hunger inside my soul to experience his love for me and to be in his presence. I yearned to hear from him that I might be transformed by his Word, by prayer, and through other Christians. When I read George Mueller's autobiography, it dawned on me that the great evangelists and missionaries of God ministered from a vibrant relationship with Jesus. Mueller wrote,

> It often now astonishes me that I did not sooner see this. In no book did I ever read about it. No public ministry ever brought the matter before me. No private intercourse with a brother stirred me up to this matter. And yet now, since God has taught me this point, it is as plain to me as anything, that the first thing the child of God has to do morning by morning is to obtain food for his inner person.[6]

For the first years of my life as a disciple, much of my energy and efforts were inward-focused. I didn't have big dreams about ministry or a plan to reach people. I didn't know there was an entire Christian subculture that made much of celebrity ministers. I certainly didn't want to change the world. I was too busy trying to fight old habits of sin and to be loyal to Jesus. I was a thirsty and needy sinner who suddenly found himself in a relationship with God. I had no idea that this was an important developmental stage.

Twenty-four years later, I look back fondly on those foundational years. On my most challenging days of pastoring a church, I remember that all this ministry began because God initiated our love relationship. As I walk with people through pain, make hard leadership decisions, prepare sermons, lead growing teams of leaders, balance budgets, and find myself in many meetings, I catch myself thinking, *I didn't sign up for all of this.* What happened to the days when my main focus was on prayer, the Word, and fellowship with God and his people?

On a human level, we all grow up, and like the Lord said to Peter, the Spirit will take us places we don't want to go (John 21:18). Becoming a mature leader in Jesus sometimes means we have leadership responsibilities that we don't like, but we must fight for faith and our love relationship. The Lord grows us through testing and response patterns. As Darrell Johnson reminds us, during these times of pressure, "a test is something meant to prove a person's character, and in the end improve it."[7]

INNER-LIFE GROWTH

Why begin an evangelism book with a chapter focused on the inner life? I believe there is an order to our process of discipleship. First, we're called to abide in Jesus, then we bear fruit. We are called to faith in God, then we are called to mission. When we confuse this sovereignly designed order, we run into deep spiritual problems. If we are new converts, we must learn to love God and begin to lay a foundation for our inner life. If we're new to the ministry, we must learn to hear from God and allow him to mature us and mentor us with wisdom, perspective, and love. If we're veterans to Christian service, we need to abide in Jesus all the more, feeding on the bread of life to address the challenges of aging, discouragements, and living fruitful lives.

God doesn't need us to be evangelists. He didn't need the 72, and he doesn't need us to change the world. Jesus could have given one word to each village, and like Lazarus, everyone who heard would have risen and begun walking in new life. He didn't choose to do this. Instead, he called seventy-two faithful disciples to experience more of the Father and his kingdom through costly and sacrificial crosscultural evangelism. Evangelism is a grace and a means for more grace for those who keep their souls happy in God.

Today I fear that if Luke were to look in on the spiritual rhythms of disciples of Jesus, he wouldn't even have a category for our approach to the Bible. We live our lives at a frenetic pace and have trouble slowing down. We don't embrace the teaching of Scripture by passionately keeping the sabbath. We run, run, run, and then run some more, without stopping to assess the effect on our souls.

We try to fit the Word in where we can, as if it were an inspiration smoothie that could provide a boost of energy. Far too often, those of us who are committed to the Word listen on the run, catching what we can on the go, maybe pulling up an application on our phone. (I have never met a deep student of God's Word who studied the Bible on a phone.) We must break through the roof, repent, and build our lives on the truth of God.

THE LIGHT

My father loved to play chess. He and his friend Carl Fabrizio sat for hours at a chess table, moving skillfully crafted jade pieces around the board. They would start in the day and end late in the evening. My father's chess lamp glowed, reflecting warm light in the entire room. For hours on end, I watched their every move. Watching them play chess was the best entertainment I could find, although I didn't understand the intricacies of the game; I often referred to the game as "check." Dad pushed the boundaries, often engaging in low-level trash talk. "C'mon, Carl. Make a move. Are you thinking about your laundry?"

Immediately after Dad's accident, a friend of my mother suggested that we call a pastor to help us. We were desperate, so Mom agreed. Four days after the crash, my very large extended family gathered at our home. Mom brought all five of her brothers from Korea to Los Angeles, and I had grown up with fifteen cousins living within five minutes of each other. On that evening, my relatives poured into the living room, and tears poured from their eyes. Aunts, uncles, and even my cousins wore black clothing, and no one said a word. The pastor opened his mouth and began to pray in Korean.

As the words of the pastor rose to heaven, a miracle came down. Though the chess lamp was off, it began to buzz without human interference. The light burned brightly during the prayer and then turned off when the prayer ended. I didn't have any language to frame what I had experienced, but I knew that something meaningful and mysterious had happened.

Many years have passed since that night. My cousins and I have all grown up. The children that wore black and mourned the death of my father now have their own spouses and children. We still gather to celebrate Christmas, and I recently brought up "the light that never goes out" experience. To a person, they all remember the pastor praying, the lamp turning on, and how it made them feel. As a family, we had experienced a bona fide miracle.

In the movie *Pulp Fiction*, two hit men debate whether or not they actually saw a miracle. Samuel L. Jackson's character says that it doesn't matter if "God stopped the bullets, or he changed Coke into Pepsi. . . . What is significant is that I felt God's touch. God got involved."[8] After the light was turned off during the wake for my father, my many fears were gone. For some strange reason, I thought that our devastated family would somehow make it. Something had gotten involved. Little did I know that something was actually Someone. Little did I know that the flickering lamp would begin my love relationship with God.

Recently, the words from Anglican author Thomas Smail's *The Forgotten Father* have renewed my passion to pursue God by building my life on his Word.

I never knew my own father; he died when I was too young to realize what I had lost, but I have been discovering slowly ever since. We are all shaped by our lacks as much as by our gifts, for none of us starts complete. One of the functions of theology is to help us test the quality of the water, to distinguish what is dead from what is alive. What I write is the theology of a grown-up boy, who in the middle of life became very conscious that he had no father, and who therefore has become full of joy in realizing that he has always had a Father God.[9]

As we move deeper into Jesus sending out his 72, I want you to know that all of ministry is to flow out of our relationship with the Father.

There is to be an order to the development of our spiritual lives: faith first, then mission.

2

SENT TO THE POOR

Most people think they are living incarnationally.
But in reality, they are just living in cars.

RAY BAKKE

BECKY WILL TAKE CARE OF ME

After months of preparation, the FOL Family Center was ready to love and serve children and families in West Long Beach. Becky and her team had carefully researched the needs. Our hearts were troubled by the fact that 65 percent of students in our ZIP code dropped out of high school after falling behind by a grade level in math or reading in elementary school. We had to do something to address the issue, because gangs, drugs, violence, and early pregnancy often awaited those who fell behind in their studies. We read books and learned about the differences between urban and suburban education. These books informed our thoughts on the ministry of the Family Center.

The phrase "we come from humble beginnings" couldn't be a more accurate depiction of our ministry. The Family Center began while we were developing our church's core group. Our new ministries were just forming, and our Life Groups (Bible studies) were in the very beginning stage. We hadn't yet begun to meet for weekly Sunday worship. Because we felt that the need was great, we began to prepare to tutor kindergarten through fifth-grade kids who needed help and encouragement.

Becky and Carol Sato (my mother-in-law and one of our founding FOL staff members) blanketed the local school with flyers announcing the new tutoring program. On the opening day, we expected one or two dozen kids to walk through the door, but no one came. The second day was empty as well. On the last day of the week, the Lord brought our first student, and she was our only student for the entire month. It was as though the Lord was personally directing the traffic flow, holding back others so we could focus, learn, and understand how much he loves the children in our neighborhood.

Kyra was a fourth grader with a D average. She had bright eyes, a spunky spirit, and was woefully behind in math and reading. Since she was the only student in the program for those first weeks, she had a unique helicopter mom/grandmother deluxe tutoring experience. Kyra learned a lot with Becky and Mom and even shared how cool it was to have Asian tutors. One hurdle we had to overcome was Kyra's five-finger-discount struggle. In two months, she "accidentally" stole Becky's phone three times. But she was still young enough to answer the phone every time I called, so we would go to her home to retrieve it.

Over the course of that semester, Kyra's marks improved dramatically. She went from a D average to a high B. The input and the love were having a great impact. The improvement was so dramatic that her teacher took her into the principal's office, and they asked Kyra what had changed for her. Without missing a beat she said, "I go to the Family Center."

Kyra had a difficult family situation. Her mother was trying to survive in the raging seas of addiction and poverty. One Friday night at around nine, we heard a knock on the door. When I opened the door, Kyra burst through and ran to Becky. Standing before me was a middle-aged African American nurse. Driving by on the main street in our neighborhood, she had seen a little girl crying near the bus stop, so she pulled over and asked her if she needed a ride. Kyra had five dollars and an address. Her mom had wanted her to take two buses to meet her at a party across town. Kyra had gotten into the nurse's car, and when the nurse asked where to take her, she wiped the tears from her eyes and said, "Please take me to Becky. She will take care of me."

After telling the story to this point, the nurse paused and said, "My name is Esther. Who are you guys?" With a deep sense of gratitude for all God had done to lead us to plant a church in West Long Beach, I said, "We are the local church."

"If you're the kind of church that loves little girls and opens up your home on a Friday night, that's the kind of church I want to be a part of," she said. The next Tuesday night, Esther was in our small-group Bible study because Kyra told her that Becky would take care of her.

We will always remember that God brought Kyra as the first of many students at the Family Center.

CHAPTER THEME: Luke's Gospel calls us to live as the 72, with and for the poor.

CORE TEXT: Luke 4:16-21

And he came to Nazareth, where he had been brought up. And as was his custom, he went to the synagogue on the Sabbath day, and he stood up to read. And the scroll of the prophet Isaiah was given to him. He unrolled the scroll and found the place where it was written,

"The Spirit of the Lord is upon me,
*   because he has anointed me*
*   to proclaim good news to the poor.*

He has sent me to proclaim liberty to the captives
and recovering of sight to the blind,
to set at liberty those who are oppressed,
to proclaim the year of the Lord's favor."

And he rolled up the scroll and gave it back to the attendant and
sat down. And the eyes of all in the synagogue were fixed on him.
And he began to say to them, "Today this Scripture has been fulfilled
in your hearing."

While every chapter is grounded in the text of Luke 10, this book emphasizes the theological call and implications of the 72 mission lifestyle. The Reverend Dr. Martin Luther King Jr. indicted the American church's understanding of race and unity with these famous words: "We must face the sad fact that at eleven o'clock on Sunday morning when we stand to sing 'In Christ there is no East or West,' we stand in the most segregated hour of America."[1] The struggles that Dr. King diagnosed have not magically disappeared. In fact, there are many today who would say that things have grown worse and the church has never been more divided.

To solve our deepest problems, we must dive deeper into Scripture. To put it plainly, the massive gaps between races, cultures, and economic classes are in opposition to the New Testament vision of a reconciled and reconciling church. The fourth chapter of Luke, the illustration of Luke 10, and the warning of Luke 16 present a very challenging call for church outreach and life together. The definition of Christian mission and community is the vision of healing for our fractured nation. We reject and deny the truth of Scripture at our own peril.

Mary's Song (Luke 1:46-56), known to the church as "The Magnificat," is the theological foundation upon which Jesus built his mission declaration (4:16-21). The song sprang forth immediately after the angel Gabriel revealed the teenager's unique role in the great plans of God. The living God has always chosen unlikely disciples, such as Abram, Sarai, Moses, Esther, and David. Mary's selection is unlike any other. The great preacher G. Campbell Morgan helps us feel the shock: "So here the messenger came, not to Judea, not to Jerusalem, not to the Temple; but to a home, on the level of the ordinary, to a despised town, and rightly despised because of its corruption; and to Galilee, held in contempt by the people of privilege; and to one woman walking in fellowship with God."[2]

Upon hearing the words of the angel, Mary was filled with the Holy Spirit and, like Hannah before her (1 Samuel 2:1-10), she responded to God's overwhelming grace in song. The structure of the song moves from Mary's personal relationship with God (Luke 1:48-50) to the larger focus of God working in and through Israel (vv. 51-54). The song speaks of two characteristics that highlight the duality of God's nature: mercy and might. The Lord is merciful, kind, and gracious to the lowly. His promise is to lift them up and feed them (v. 53). But to the proud, the powerful, and the rich, he is just. His promise is to bring them down and send them away empty-handed (v. 53). The song is full of revolutionary language denoting God's commitment to fight for the vulnerable of the world. Joel Green fills out the implication of this text for us: "God, the Divine Warrior, makes war with the rulers of the world. His opponents are those who grasp for social respect and enjoy power, excluding the less fortunate and socially unacceptable. This is not to say this is God's last word for them."[3]

From the very beginning of the third Gospel, God has aligned himself with the poor, just as he has from the beginning of Scripture.

Mary's Song is at the very heart of the Christian faith. It is Luke's declaration of God's purposes in our world today. The rest of the book adds flesh to the song. We see the mercy and might of God play out in interactions with widows, Gentiles, the sick, and the demonized. In parables, Jesus warned about sitting too far up, lest you be thrown down. In other teaching, he warned about the corrosive nature of wealth, luxury, and status. It's no wonder the great missionary E. Stanley Jones stated, "The Magnificat is the most revolutionary document in the history of the world."[4]

God choosing sides with the poor forces the proud, powerful, and rich to also choose the poor if they are to align themselves with God. Anything less and they are on the opposite side of God and his purposes. The revolution has begun.

THE FIRST SERMON

Chapter four is the theological center of Luke's Gospel. Jesus teaching in his hometown, the Nazarene *barrio* of Capernaum, is Luke's first account of his public speaking ministry. It is the first sermon attributed to Jesus in the third Gospel, and it serves not only as a first chronologically but also in terms of purpose and definition. Respected author and first-century culture expert Kenneth Bailey affirms the centrality of this sermon: "The most detailed account of the inauguration of Jesus' public ministry is recorded in Luke 4:16-31. This rich and densely packed passage merits an attempt to unlock at least a few of its secrets."[5]

As with any great historical leader, Jesus' first public address set the tone and established the vision for future ministry. As he unwrapped the scroll of Isaiah and began to teach in the local synagogue, who could have imagined that what he would say would turn the world upside down? Two thousand years later, he is still at work to turn our own lives upside down, that we might further align ourselves with the poor.

With fire in his eyes and authority in his voice, Jesus declared that Father, Son, and Spirit are all about the preaching of the gospel to the poor. The Father sent him to liberate the captives. The Spirit anointed him to preach the good news. And he, the Son, came to earth to execute the plan. References to those in need in Luke, including the word *poor*, are made ten times. Preaching the gospel to the poor and lifting up the lowly are not good ideas or unintended results: they are the central plan.

If we were present in the synagogue that day, the word *poor* would have contextual meaning. In first-century Mediterranean culture, poverty was not just economic. It was an Asian culture that centered on status, honor, and shame. Five central characteristics would cause someone to be placed in the "poor" classification in first-century Israel:

- economics: those without material resources
- vocation: those with immoral jobs (tax collectors, prostitutes)
- gender: women in that patriarchal society
- health: those who were diseased or demonized
- race: Gentiles were considered poor

I like to exchange the word *vulnerable* for the word *poor*. I believe that our concept of those in need should emphasize their experience and lifestyle, not only their economic reality. The poor in our culture today are often looked down upon. Questions about why they are poor and what bad decisions they've made creep into our discussions. It's interesting that Jesus didn't qualify his statement that "the poor" was the demographic of people he had come to bless.

As the vulnerable among us struggle, do they know that Jesus came for them? As the vulnerable among us cry, do they know that Jesus wipes away tears? As the vulnerable among us starve and thirst, are they aware that Jesus has physical and spiritual food and water?

The Father sent Jesus to make disciples among the poor. The Spirit anointed Jesus to preach the good news to those on the margins.

THE SERMON RESPONSE

This vision was initially well received (Luke 4:22). The reaction only proved that his hearers, likely moral and upstanding Jews, weren't classified as "poor" in first-century Mediterranean culture. If they understood the heart of Jesus' teaching and its implications for their lives, they would have felt threatened and come out swinging. But they applauded politely as though at a piano recital.

Jesus took them deeper with two illustrations that grabbed their attention and caused their blood to boil. Of the voluminous material he could have cited to show God's work as recorded in the Old Testament, he chose Yahweh sending Elijah to the widow at Zarephath (4:26) and Elisha ministering to Naaman, the Syrian leper (4:27). In both examples, Jesus highlighted that the beneficiaries of God's grace were far outside the dominant system. The recipients of God's kindness were of a different culture and class than Israel.

Through the anointing of the Holy Spirit (4:18), Jesus was creating a new society, not based on culture or class, but on faith and the eternal values of the kingdom of God. In this kingdom, tax collectors became Gospel authors, a woman at a well became a spiritual well for her entire village, and murderers became apostles and church planters. In this kingdom, the most vulnerable received the greatest care.

South African missiologist David Bosch highlighted the centrality of Jesus' blessing those on the margins, saying, "If we did not have Luke, we would have probably lost an important, if not the most, part of the earliest Christian tradition and its intense preoccupation with the figure and message of Jesus as the hope of the poor."[6]

Is this good news? Well, it all depends on how we see ourselves. If we're willing to align our lives with God as he lifts the needy, marginalized, and vulnerable, this is great news. We will love being invited to participate in Jesus' mission. If, however, we cherish our places of power and refuse to enter into sacrificial mission on behalf of the poor, we will reject the mission in order to attempt to save our own lives.

The first hearers were clearly in the camp of people who wanted to hold on to their status and lifestyle. Like frequent flyers who suddenly hear that their point system has changed, they reacted strongly. They didn't write calm, calculated letters to executives or rant on social media. They were so offended that they began to insult Jesus and his mother, demand a paternity test, and attempt to kill him. Their reaction reveals how far from God and his priorities they had drifted into their place of privilege. John Perkins reminds us that reconciliation is the central goal of the gospel.

> The only purpose of the gospel is to reconcile people to God and to each other. A gospel that does not reconcile is not a Christian gospel at all. But in America it seems as if we don't believe that. We don't really believe that the proof of our discipleship is that we love one another (John 13:35). No, we think the proof is in numbers—church attendance, decision cards. Even if our "converts" continue to hate each other, even if they will not worship with the brothers and sisters in Christ, we point to their "conversion" as evidence of the gospel's success. We have substituted a gospel of church growth for a gospel of reconciliation.
>
> And how convenient it is that our "church growth experts" tell us that homogenous churches grow fastest! That welcome news seems to relieve us of the responsibility to overcome

racial barriers in our churches. It seems to justify not bothering with breaking down racial barriers, since that would only distract us from "church growth." And so the most segregated racist institution in America, the evangelical church, racks up the numbers, declaring itself "successful," oblivious to the fact that this dismemberment of the Body of Christ broadcasts to the world every day a hypocrisy as blatant as Peter's at Antioch—a living denial of the truth of the gospel.[7]

When we extend the vision of Jesus' first sermon to its fruition, I believe the fulfillment is multiethnic and multiclass communities of faith. The coming of God's kingdom brings together that which separates us in our world today: race and economics.

THE CONTEXT OF THE 72 CALL

As we consider the call and training of the 72, we must remember that this evangelism training day didn't occur independently from what came before in the third gospel. The events of Luke 10 build on the first nine chapters of the book. I fear our defaults in biblical interpretation are random Bible studies, proof-texting the Scriptures, and topical sermons. Christian philosopher and author Dallas Willard expounded on what happens when the teachers of God do not go deep into God's Word to feed the sheep:

> Should we not at least consider the possibility that this poor result [today's weak churches] is not in spite of what we teach and how we teach, but precisely because of it? Might that not lead to our discerning why the power of Jesus and his gospel has been cut off from ordinary human existence, leaving it adrift from the flow of his eternal kind of life?[8]

It's far easier to live out Luke 10 once it has been removed from Luke 4. If Luke 10 were an isolated text, I believe that almost all our evangelism would be with people who are just like us. The church-growth movement was built on the premise that the gospel reaches people more rapidly when shared across the same culture and class lines. While it might be strategically accurate, it misses the centrality of the gospel's power to reconcile across culture and class.

While we know little about the 72, we can infer from the context that they were Jewish converts (Jesus' teaching had not yet gone to Gentiles) who followed Jesus, his vision, and his rules of the kingdom. We don't know if they were wealthy and powerful (insiders) or if they were poor and marginalized (outsiders). We do know that the call of the gospel was for each one of the 72 to initiate and love those who were different from them in culture and class.

To be quite honest, the results of living out this vision are abysmal, and so we find ourselves with churches that are defined by cultural affinity and economic status. The exemplary work of Curtiss DeYoung and his coauthors revealed that a mere 8.5 percent of 300,000 American churches were multiethnic. Of those 25,000 multiethnic churches, only 6 percent were multiclass.[9] This leaves a depressing figure of 1,500 churches out of 300,000 that are designed with the core vision of the third Gospel.

The 72 were faithful and functional. I don't believe they were the destitute poor. There were some who likely came from modest or poor backgrounds, but the teachings of Luke 4 don't disqualify the poor from loving those on the margins. Those in poverty can also find someone who is of a different culture and/or more marginalized than they are.

If we read the Luke 10 call to witness and we assume that God wants us to reach people who are just like us, we miss the rest of the context of Luke's Gospel. Christian phrases like "grow where you are planted" spiritualize and justify decisions to avoid crossing the barriers of culture and class. Jesus sends the 72 as an extension of the vision to bring his good news to the poor. Yet I fear that because of such a shallow biblical understanding and an unwillingness to give up our safe and comfortable lifestyles, we do the opposite of what Jesus requires.

LOCATION! LOCATION! LOCATION!

When Becky and I were invited to go through an assessment process for church planters, we participated in a group simulation. With church planting assessors observing us with eagle eyes, we were given an assignment to create a ministry plan to plant ten churches in ten years in a major American city. It was fascinating to see the apostolic gift rising in many of us. We agreed that we should plant a flagship church that would inspire, model, and create resources for the next nine.

The simulation turned contentious when we discussed where to plant the first new church. The four other couples immediately drew a big red circle in the most resourced, stable, growing, comfortable, and luxurious part of town. They argued that in order to reach the city, we needed to reach its wealthy and its leaders. They quoted a very popular Christian book to back up the claim that this was the most strategic model for effective church planting. And it is, if the goal is to reach the wealthy and privileged of society.

Becky and I drew a big red circle in the lowest-income neighborhood. We argued that if you choose to plant a church in the hood, you can call the rich of the city to join the crosscultural mission. If you begin with the poor, you have an opportunity to disciple the poor and rich. If you start with the rich, you lose the poor, because not many people have the resources to travel or feel comfortable in wealthier settings. Becky and I quoted the book of Luke, not the popular Christian book promoting church growth. We were met with blank stares and a few contentious comments. We were glad they didn't take us up the mountain to try to throw us off a cliff.

The call of the 72 wasn't merely evangelists doing evangelism. The 72 were trained to do evangelism among the poor.

WEST LONG BEACH

The city of Long Beach, nestled in the southernmost tip of Los Angeles County, is home to nearly six hundred thousand people with over thirty-eight distinct neighborhoods. The shoreline is an impressive and luxurious destination for many people. Boasting homes that are priced in the millions of dollars, the Naples and oceanfront areas of Long Beach offer a life of beauty and luxury.

In the late 1930s and 1940s, thousands of Americans from the Midwest and mid-South packed up their belongings and moved west. In the 1950s, Long Beach was featured in one of Elvis Presley's films, *The Dust Bowl Migration*. In the 1970s, Long Beach saw another wave of immigrants from Southeast Asia. Cambodians arrived there, and many made their homes and created businesses along Anaheim Street. Today Long Beach is home to more Cambodians than any other city in the world, except Phnom Penh, Cambodia's capital.

To handle the massive number of new residents moving into Long Beach, city planners and the local government saw fit to relocate many poor people into West Long Beach. The Springdale West Apartments housing project was built with 410 units and over 2,500 residents. While there are many upstanding citizens, there are others in the complex who choose to make life dangerous for the other residents. Each apartment has a gigantic number painted on the roof so police helicopters can inform officers on the ground which apartment to run toward in the event of a crisis or criminal activity. The *Long Beach Press Telegram* once ran a cover story on Springdale with the following catch line: "If the West Coast Crips gang had a headquarters, it would be here, at the Springdale West apartments."[10]

The average household income in West Long Beach hovers around $37,500. Most of our neighbors are hardworking, family-oriented, and providing for their families through jobs in the service sector, doing their best to keep it all together while laying a foundation for their children and extended families. A large percentage of their limited resources goes to housing. There are too many people crammed into too-small apartments.

Our neighborhood has many iconic inner-city benchmarks. Sometimes shoes hang from the telephone wires, announcing that drug dealers are open for business. The ice-cream truck has long lines of adults at nine in the evening. On the first and last Friday of the month, our local market has lines out the door of single mothers wiring money to their men, who are in jail. Graffiti appears on fences, walls, and driveways, and young boys ride away on their bikes with spray-paint cans popping out of their oversize jeans.

My mom was an elementary school teacher for forty-five years. As I grew up, valuing education was like breathing, Korean food, and Dodgers baseball. So it was the big red flag when we began to learn about West Long Beach schools. Local schools were underperforming, including Webster Elementary, our home school, which had academic test scores that ranked among the lowest in the city. The system produces expected results. Funding for public schools is tied to property tax value. This promotes an unjust systemic policy ensuring that neighborhoods with the best homes have the best schools.

While we were aware of these challenges secondhand, the experience of sending our own children into the same schools was very different. Becky and I have chosen to make West Long Beach our mission field. We have chosen to make the problems of the city our problems. We have chosen to make the schools in West Long Beach our schools. And we have chosen to plant our church in West Long Beach, believing that the mission of God is to create new communities of faith that are multiethnic and multiclass.

In chapter five, we'll explore friendships and the ministry goal of building trust with nonbelievers. It's important to provide a preview of that theme as it relates to the poor.

Evangelism today sinks or swims based on the strength of relationships. The way to build trust with people is to have strong friendships. How will we win those who are different from us if we have no relationships? How will we make and deepen disciples among the urban poor if they're not our friends first? Where you live and who you do life with determines the nature of the spiritual fruit in your ministry.

Location is everything as you live the vision of the 72.

JORGE

I first met Jorge in a hallway at Webster Elementary School. Our girls were in the same transitional kindergarten class. We'd always see each other walking up and down the hallway but rarely would he return my "What's up?" His tattoos and clothing indicated that he had an extensive gang background. On one occasion, I saw him blow up in the hall at his daughter's teacher. I could tell he didn't want to have this conflict, but it had happened. He seemed like a troubled soul. He was a perfect candidate for a 72 relationship.

A breakthrough in our friendship came during the NFL playoffs. His team, the Raiders, had won a very big game. He was excited to talk about the defense, the incredible wide receiver Amari Cooper, and the upcoming playoff game. I was very glad for our connection and that we were building trust. I prayed for Jorge and asked God to move our friendship from secular to sacred.

On Valentine's Day, I was in my morning prayer, and I lifted Jorge up to the living God. As I prayed for him, I heard the Holy Spirit say to me, "Take Jorge Korean food." When I saw him in the school hallway, I told him I wanted to share my culture and bring over some Korean food to his house. He gave me his address and said that would be cool.

When I pulled up to the address, his block was very active. The empty street looked like a set from a gang movie without any actors. I knocked on the door, and Jorge greeted me. He said that he was surprised that I'd kept my word, because so few people do anymore. I nodded and began to share with him why Korean food is the most delicious food in the world.

Jorge was quiet, and then he looked me in the eye as if he really wanted to communicate something important. He said to me, "I really appreciate you doing this. Today is my birthday, and this is a really special gift."

I told him how God had told me earlier that morning that I was supposed to bring him Korean food. I shared with him that God was real, loved him deeply, and because of that love had sent me to be a spiritual blessing in his life. I asked him if he would consider Bible study. He quickly said yes and added, "I am a man of my word." I prayed for him and asked God to bless him on his birthday.

For the next three months, Jorge faithfully attended Bible study, Sunday worship, and even a Lakers game with my best friend, Isaac Flores, and me. On Easter Sunday, Jorge made a commitment to become a disciple of Jesus. He eventually joined the mission force as one of the West Long Beach 72.

THE WAY UP IS DOWN

I had the honor of officiating a friend's wedding at a world-class hotel in a very wealthy Orange County beach community. When Becky and I sat down for the wedding meal, we began to get to know some of the people around the table. One couple seemed particularly interested in our church plant. They asked us many questions about the life of our church, and their eyes lit up as we talked. They said they were Christians and were searching for a church that was Bible-centered, evangelistic, multicultural, and multiclass. We affirmed their desire to live out the values of the kingdom. "John and Becky, we love everything we hear about FOL," said the wealthy businessman. "Would you consider moving your church to Laguna Hills so we can be a part of it?" Our jaws almost dropped as the words left his mouth.

On the drive home, Becky and I debriefed the conversation. We discussed how their question had disregarded so much of God's work in our lives over the last twenty years. Their request to move the church to their city also disregarded the neighbors we love. It became clear that in their minds, moving to the beach would be a great promotion or some kind of spiritual upgrade for us. They didn't have eyes to see that by embracing the urban poor, we had become rich in the things of the kingdom of God. "Do they think we just happened to end up in West Long Beach?" Becky asked. "They don't realize that we have chosen—and continue to choose—West Long Beach."

We don't often reflect on how much our choices have an impact on the lives of our children. We are thankful that our oldest daughter, Joy, has a keen eye, a sensitive heart, and a flair for action to help meet the practical needs around her. One morning when she was in fifth grade, a deluge hit West Long Beach. There were puddles everywhere, and the streets were partially flooded.

At Webster Elementary, many of the children weren't prepared, and they slogged around all day in their wet socks. The next day, as the storm persisted, Joy decided to bless her friends. She began to ask questions, and it turned out many of them had only one pair of socks.

Her teacher, Mrs. Elaine Powers, a strong Christian and powerful woman of prayer, called to tell us that Joy had stuffed her entire backpack with socks, and she had given them all to her friends. The 72, even fifth-grade girls, can help heal the wounds of poverty by living out the gospel and sharing God's abundant resources.

The way up is down in the kingdom of God. If Mary's Song is true, on that great day the Lord will literally turn the world upside down. Those who have positioned themselves at the top of the world will experience a shocking and horrific fall. But the Lord himself will lift up those who have positioned themselves in faith with the lowly.

Will you be on the right side when the great turn takes place? Who will be the direct beneficiaries of your discipleship? Are you befriending, engaging, and loving those who are just like you, while ignoring the needs of those on the margins? If so, I wonder if the apostle Luke might be tempted to say, "Even sinners do that."

Yes, the way up is down in the kingdom of God.

WOLVES, BEARS, AND CRUSHING PRESSURE

It is good to wrestle for divine blessings.

DAVID BRAINERD

HOW IS TOM SMITH DOING?

My wonderful mother, Yung Soon Teter, passed away on February 26, 2016, at the age of eighty-six. For the last season of her life, she lived with our family. It was our joy to care for her, watch her play with the grandchildren, and celebrate her life. During her final years, her memory betrayed her. She suffered from age-related dementia, remembering people and places, but most recent events eluded her.

I learned so much about my mom during this final season. The doctors warned us that when this type of dementia kicks in, it often causes frustration for the sufferer. She warned us that Mom could internalize frustration because her brain was no longer functioning correctly. She could be very hard on herself and those around her. The doctor also said that the condition helps bring out the true self, since some of the inhibitions and filters are removed. We embraced the moment and prepared for a cranky version of Mom.

As time progressed, we were pleasantly surprised at how sweet Mom's personality and disposition were. She would make the children laugh and sing, and they played the flute with her. She never complained and was always quick with a compliment. Some days, she would ask our church staff the same question many times in an hour. And she always asked me the same question: "How is Tom Smith doing?"

Tom Smith was my junior tennis coach. I began private lessons when I was ten, and he was a great grace in my life, especially after my father's sudden death when I was eleven. He had been a college tennis player, a professional on the tour for a season or three, and was an excellent coach. He taught me the fundamentals of the game and drilled into me that serving and returning are at least 50 percent of all match play. He carefully taught me the mechanics of the four serves needed to compete at a high level: flat serve up the middle, cut serve out wide, block serve to the body, and the "American twist" for my second serves. With these serves in my arsenal, I began to play competitively and enjoyed some early success.

Thirty years later, I fondly remember the multiple hours on the tennis court with Tom and my mom. She was a part of every lesson and always went out of her way to help pick up the balls. She laughed when Tom told me, "Your serve is pretty good for a short dude." And he would always say to Mom, "Yung Soon, John is going to make me rich and famous one day." Today I always pass that line on to my children as I teach them the game. I hope it makes them feel as good as it did me.

In the summer of 1982, I was twelve and competing in a national junior tennis tournament. The local winners would advance to regionals, and the regional winners were invited to the national final in New York City, held during the US Open. I breezed through the local tournament. The next step was battling tennis players from all over the West Coast at the UCLA tennis center. The college was huge to a preteen boy, and the venue was overwhelming. There were so many good junior tennis players from Southern California to Las Vegas to Seattle. And there were so many people watching.

Though my tournament was thirty-five years ago, I can almost feel the butterflies in my stomach and the knocking in my knees when I was called to my first match of the day. Tom had prepared me well. Knowing that the pressure would be great, he taught me phrases to remember during tough games: "I know how to play the game." When the pressure was greatest, Tom taught me to say to myself, "John, focus on fundamentals."

At the beginning of my first match, I won the coin toss and elected to serve. That tennis ball felt like a medicine ball, and my Kennex Black racket felt like a fifty-pound club. I breathed, gathered myself, bounced the ball five times, and acted, because I knew how to play the game. My first serve was a cutter to his forehand, and the ball kept running away from my opponent. I won the first point. I ended up winning the match—and the next match as well. I was suddenly in the finals.

The pressure only increased at the end of the day. My opponent and I were both exhausted as we played for the right to advance to New York. I focused on the fundamentals, and I was able to execute under pressure. I will never forget the elation and sense of relief when my opponent's last shot sailed wide. I was going to New York City.

NEW YORK CITY, AUGUST 1992

My mom and I flew together to New York. I played in the tournament and lost in the quarterfinals, but the memories of that week will last forever. We met Arthur Ashe at the tournament's opening. Mom spoke to Jimmy Connors on an outside court and even got a really bad picture of his backside as he was warming up. (There were no iPhones or selfies back in the day.) We were in the front row to watch John McEnroe play a late-night fourth-round match. Mom and I took the subway back to the players' hotel at one in the morning.

We even got to climb up to the top of the Statue of Liberty together. I felt like Jay Z, sitting courtside high-fiving Nets and Knicks, "close enough to trip a referee."[1]

The week Mom and I spent together in New York is one of my life highlights. This grace came one year after I lost my dad and she her husband of twenty-eight years. This joy was deposited so deep in her soul, it eluded the dementia.

I so wish I could hear Mom ask me one more time, "How is Tom Smith doing?" I haven't seen Tom in thirty years, but I hope to find him. I want to thank him for teaching me to play the game. And I want to thank him for training me to handle crushing pressure. Without Tom, Mom and I would never have seen New York City together.

Tom prepared me for a tennis tournament, but Jesus trained his seventy-two evangelists for a more challenging event. When Jesus trained the 72, his method and content assumed that his disciples would compete and execute under crushing pressure.

CHAPTER THEME: Jesus trains the 72 for evangelism under crushing pressure.

CORE TEXT: Overview of Luke 10:10-16

> "But whenever you enter a town and they do not receive you, go into its streets and say, 'Even the dust of your town that clings to our feet we wipe off against you. Nevertheless know this, that the kingdom of God has come near.' I tell you, it will be more bearable on that day for Sodom than for that town.

*"Woe to you, Chorazin! Woe to you, Bethsaida! For if the mighty
works done in you had been done in Tyre and Sidon, they would
have repented long ago, sitting in sackcloth and ashes. But it will be
more bearable in the judgment for Tyre and Sidon than for you. And
you, Capernaum, will you be exalted to heaven? You shall be brought
down to Hades.*

*"The one who hears you hears me, and the one who rejects you
rejects me, and the one who rejects me rejects him who sent me."*

Jesus trained the 72 for their mission in an intentional and me-
thodical way. He carefully taught them the nuts and bolts of how
to share their faith. The second half of this book will focus on the
ministry skills we need to live out the vision of the 72 in our ministry contexts.

Three core tasks make up the 72 lifestyle: (1) earnest prayers,
(2) moving our friendships from secular to sacred, (3) and helping
our friends hear the gospel and be healed by the gospel. For the
72, this was their ministry action plan. Each of these evangelism
tasks rightly deserves its own chapter. The technical steps of
sharing our faith have been the subject of innumerable books and
even more plenary sessions at conferences. Yet this is only half of
the training agenda. In Luke 10:1-9, Luke wrote seven verses that
are instructive. (I don't include his opening statement [v. 1] or
Jesus' pastoral framing of how they would feel like sheep among
wolves [v. 3].) Jesus identified what the 72 needed to *do* in their
evangelism and put together the curriculum in seven verses.

As the training continues, there are exactly another seven
verses—Luke 10:10-16—dedicated to how the 72 will experience
rejection. Isn't it remarkable that there are the same number of
verses for how to handle spurning and spite as there are for proactive things we must do to win people for the kingdom? I have
been to many evangelism training conferences. I can't recall ever

hearing a sermon solely dedicated to persecution and rejection. I've certainly never seen balanced input on ministry skills and suffering that resembled Jesus' training agenda. And yet he saw fit to make that an essential preparation element for his 72.

Jesus fully expected his disciples to suffer rejection. Therefore we must make certain that we are likewise prepared for rejection and persecution. To be powerful, the 72 needed to have the mindset that they would suffer. Since the Lord Jesus has placed such a high value on understanding these issues, let's work through Luke 10:10-16 by identifying the driving force behind persecution and then ask four questions of the text.

THLIPSIS TRAINING

The Greek word *thlipsis* is translated as "tribulation." The word appears sixteen times in the New Testament. Jesus and the New Testament authors used it to describe the burdens associated with the coming of the kingdom. Thlipsis evokes the pressures that emerge when two massive objects collide. Pastor Darrell Johnson helps us understand this concept: "Thlipsis is the pressure experienced along the line where kingdoms clash; along the line where the kingdom of light clashes with the kingdom of darkness; along the line where the kingdom of justice clashes with the reign of injustice; along the line where the rule of life clashes with the rule of death."[2]

Thlipsis occurs when the evil one feels threatened by the kingdom of God coming near (10:11). When disciples go out and faithfully live and speak God's Word, the power of the Word causes red flags throughout the dark kingdom. As Jesus' Word informs, performs, and transforms, the evil army fires back. The devil and his host will not lie down willingly when the good news of the gospel causes people to believe in Jesus, to be healed, and to be freed from idols. The resulting pushback, thlipsis, occurs when two tectonic plates collide. Jesus trained his 72 to be powerful in the midst of great opposition.

Today in the West, we must understand the concept of thlipsis if we are to live out the vision of 72. Our daily frustrations don't approach the level of thlipsis. Having a bad boss and nasty co-workers is reality, not crushing pressure. The challenges of marriage, raising children, and navigating singleness are relational challenges in a sinful and fallen world. Lines at Starbucks, extreme traffic, and rude flight attendants are not thlipsis; they are the frustrations of life on planet Earth.

An entirely different dimension of suffering awaits the 72. We are called to operate on the fault lines between two colliding kingdoms. Living out the deeds of the faith of the 72 is the catalyst for this collision. Before we are sent out, there is no collision. But because our faithful and anonymous ministry partners are doing the good work of the kingdom, the dark side fires back. Thlipsis is why non-Christians fire back with persecution, gossip, and even violence. We who seek to be faithful come up against greater, harsher, and more penetrating pressure. Can you feel the pressure mounting in your own ministry context? Take heart. Jesus trained the 72 for thlipsis.

The 72 that go forth into their ministry appointment are like sheep among wolves (10:3). Clearly the Lord used this animal-kingdom metaphor to show a lesser and dominant pairing. The sheep are vulnerable because they don't have the predatory nature of the wolf; they aren't as cunning and crafty in their hunting and defense, and they are outnumbered. Enemies surround them, en-emies that want to hurt, maim, and devour. Without the shepherd standing with the sheep, protecting the sheep with the rod and staff and strategically moving them, they are vulnerable.

FIGHTING BEARS

In the film *The Revenant*, Leonardo DiCaprio plays Hugh Glass, an employee of the Rocky Mountain Fur Company. Glass and his company of traders are attacked by an Arikara tribe for the animal pelts, and fifteen of his colleagues are killed in the battle. Glass and those who are left escape into the forest near the Missouri River in what is present-day South Dakota.

While navigating the cold and the treacherous mountain terrain at age forty-three, Glass is attacked and mauled by a grizzly bear. The filmmaker, Alejandro González Iñárritu, captures the attack and Glass's survival in a horrifying sequence. The force, the vicious swiping of the bear, and Glass's enduring will to survive make the scene unforgettable.

When I hear Jesus tell the 72 they're being sent out as sheep among wolves, I take off my stained-glass lens and read what the Lord of the harvest is really saying. The image is terrifying; it should make our palms sweat and our hearts beat faster. Jesus wasn't warning the 72 that they would have people gossiping about them. He wasn't strengthening them for someone writing negative words about them on Twitter or Facebook. This was so much greater than mean tweets. He was training them to survive bear attacks.

As I write, my heart is filled with sadness for the global church. On a recent Palm Sunday, suicide bombers attacked two Christian churches in Egypt. On Easter Sunday, our brothers and sisters in Alexandria and Tanta celebrated the resurrection of Jesus a week after their pastors, family, and friends had been killed. Jesus said we will be like sheep among the wolves. Being persecuted, violated, and even murdered must fit into our 72 worldview. The 72 were powerful because they were ready to die.

FOUR QUESTIONS

To understand how the 72 were trained to be faithful evangelists in a hostile environment, let's work through four questions raised by the seven verses of Luke 10:10-16.

Why did Jesus tell the 72 to wipe the dust off their feet after being rejected (10:11)? He himself was rejected by those nearest to him and those he reached out to, and he gave the 72 clear protocols on what to do if the message of the kingdom of God was spurned. Wiping the dust from feet was an act connected to ridding oneself of defilement, such as when one had traveled to Gentile lands.[3] I also believe this teaching helped the evangelists avoid the temptation of spending too much time with people who weren't interested in the things of God. The 72 didn't have the luxury of lingering and loitering on their evangelistic journey. In dusting off their feet, they were given a powerful and easily understood cultural tool to get the attention of the hardhearted while moving the mission ahead to reach more people.

What was Jesus teaching the 72 by citing the judgment of Sodom (10:12)? Those who likely converted during Jesus' first ministry years in Capernaum would have been familiar with the Old Testament account of Sodom. The prophet Ezekiel tells us that Sodom and Gomorrah were proud cities of luxury, wealth, and injustice (Ezekiel 16:55). The Genesis account speaks of widespread sexual immorality in the cities. Sodom was famous for its lack of hospitality and its rejection of foreigners, its unrepentant attitudes, and its giving over to lusts. After many warnings, God destroyed its cities (Genesis 19:29).

Upon hearing these words of Jesus, the 72 learned much about judgment. God will not only judge individuals but also cities. Therefore, we must labor and partner with God to help our cities flourish. Author and minister William Barclay wrote, "It is a terrible thing to reject God's invitation. There is a sense in which every promise of God that a man hears will become his condemnation."[4] Jesus stressed that cities will be judged based on what they know and have experienced from God. He also promised it would be easier for the Gentile regions of Tyre and Sidon because they had experienced less of the gospel and responded in faith better than the Jewish regions, which were given a greater amount of exposure but responded with less faith.

Do we think like that with our evangelism relationships? Do we dare tell our friends who have seen the kingdom of God and tasted of its goodness that they will be judged by how they act on what they have been given? The 72 were empowered with the historical precedent of God's judgment upon individuals and even cities that reject his gospel.

Why did Jesus end this part of his talk by telling the disciples that when they were rejected, it was the Father who was being rejected (10:16)? Jesus knew the 72 would be affected by rejection. Dusting off the dirt was a prophetic word of judgment for the listener to consider and process. Jesus had modeled conflict and rejection by the religious leaders. He had brought them in on his secret by sharing his personal power base when persecution hit.

Jesus' core identity was as God's Son who had delivered the message of salvation. It wasn't his message; it was the Father's message. Jesus was but the messenger. In the same way, the 72 needed to know that their task was to deliver the message. Their work was done when the message was out. The audiences, both positive and negative, were now dealing with the One who had sent the message. The 72 had power because they understood that it was about the message and never about the messenger.

In Luke's Gospel, immediately after sharing about the cross and his own suffering, Jesus called the 72 to be his delivery people of the good news in our dark world. Though they were like sheep among wolves, they didn't lose heart. Actually, they thrived. The crushing pressure of the world drove the faithful to deeper levels of devotion, loyalty, and rejection of sin.

JOHN, YOU'RE FIRED

After graduating from UCLA, I committed to a volunteer staff position with InterVarsity Christian Fellowship. I was passionate about serving the campus, reaching lost people, and building up the campus fellowship of faith. But I needed to pay the bills, so I took a part-time job with a charity that provided services to empower those with disabilities. It was my first job since I had become a Christian a year earlier. Our eight-employee office was full of characters. I loved to share my faith, but I tried to stay within cultural norms, and I tried not to be arrogant or tone-deaf. I certainly didn't apply too much pressure.

At work, I often shared stories at the copier or asked parabolic questions during the coffee break. I spent the first few weeks trying to get to know people and gain insight into where they stood in light of Jesus and his saving gospel. Over private lunches, I asked my friends if they were interested in studying the Bible together. One person, a diehard USC Trojan who was trying to extend her sorority lifestyle postgraduation, expressed some interest. Two others were deeply offended that I would even bring up Jesus, let alone ask them if they were interested in studying the Word of God.

I soon found myself across the desk from the executive director. She warned me that I wasn't allowed to proselytize at the office. I certainly didn't think that was the word for what I was doing, but I bit my tongue. I respectfully replied that technically it was outside the office during our lunch breaks that I tried to share my faith. She had none of it and threw down a few "stop sharing your faith or else" ultimatums. I wanted to reply, "Whether it is right in the sight of God to listen to you rather than to God, you must judge, for we cannot but speak of what we have seen and heard" (Acts 4:19-20). But I certainly needed the job, or so I thought, and I chose to stand down. I don't remember if there was any great incident, but a few weeks later I was asked to leave the organization because the other employees were uncomfortable with my "active faith."

I learned an important lesson that day. If you are faithful to share Jesus, there's a good chance some will be interested and others will get angry. In the grand plans of God, I didn't need my paycheck. Jesus is the one who sustains the entire universes (Hebrews 1:3) and was certainly helping me pay the rent, keep the car moving, and have enough food and drink to survive. And that persecution made me long for full-time ministry. I didn't want to find myself across a desk from an unbeliever who knew nothing about what they were talking about. I decided then and there to become a pastor. I was pretty confident that no pastor would ever be fired for preaching the gospel.

DAVID BRAINERD

David Brainerd, one of the great evangelists of all time, proved faithful and fruitful under crushing pressure. He was born April 20, 1718. As a young man, he had a large soul for the things of God. He read through the Bible twice and was very consistent in the habit of journaling. He attended Yale University to prepare to serve God for all of his days as a pastor, but unique circumstances led him to feel as though his life calling had been terminated.

From the time he was a boy, Brainerd battled health and emotional issues. In our era, he would probably be diagnosed with clinical depression. He also battled tuberculosis, which would claim his life at the young age of twenty-nine. His twenties were filled with melancholy and a tendency toward despondency, season upon season of spitting up blood, and staring at the door that had closed his ministry dreams. But Brainerd persevered, and today he is one of the greatest among those who have lived as part of the 72.

The Lord of the harvest called Brainerd to enter into ministry in the wilderness. This was not a metaphor. He moved to the woods of New Jersey to minister to the Crossweeksung tribe. Suffering under relentless depressing, debilitating illness, extreme weather, displacement, and loneliness, Brainerd wrote in his journals of bonding with the Indians, learning their culture and language, and beginning to tell them about Jesus, only to have them mock him, beat him, and send him off alone to his hut. As one of the 72, he enjoyed few of life's pleasures. He wrote, "May, 1743: I live poorly with regard to the comforts of life: most of my diet consists of boiled corn, hasty pudding, etc. I lodge on a bundle of straw, and my labor is hard and extremely difficult; and I have little experience of success to comfort me."[5]

In the biting winters of New Jersey, Brainerd vomited blood outside the teepee, went inside for warmth, then returned outside to cough up blood again in the snow. All the while, he was breathing the smoke that further irritated his condition. Brainerd wrote in his journal, "Sunday, December 16, 1744. I was so overwhelmed with dejection that I knew not how to live: I longed for death exceedingly: My soul was 'sunk in deep waters,' and 'the floods' were ready to 'drown me': I was so much oppressed that my soul was in a kind of horror."[6]

Although Brainerd saw no converts for seven years, he remained a faithful missionary. Finally, something in the heavens broke. He wrote in his journal about the testimony of one of the converts, who went on to become one of the leaders of the new faith community in Crossweeksung: "I have many times heard you speak of the goodness and the sweetness of Christ, that he was better than all the world. But oh! I knew nothing what you meant. I never believed you! I never believed you! But now, I know it is true!"[7]

Brainerd died October 9, 1747. For seven years, he had faithfully lived out the vision of the 72. He delivered his ministry under extreme internal and external pressure. He saw Satan fall like lightning from heaven in Crossweeksung. And his impact is immeasurable. Countless missionaries since have gone into the den of wolves, armed only with their Bibles and strengthened by his journals.

The effect of Brainerd's ministry is the same as the most awesome effect of every pastor's ministry. There are a few Indians, perhaps several hundred, who owe their everlasting life to the direct love and ministry of David Brainerd. If we live twenty-nine years or if we live ninety-nine years, wouldn't any hardships be worth the saving of one person from the eternal torments of hell for the everlasting enjoyment of the glory of God?[8]

PART

2

APPLICATION

4

HOW PEOPLE
BECOME CHRISTIANS

When you find a ministry structure to effectively
deliver your ministry, work it to death.

G. CAMPBELL MORGAN

In John's Gospel, Nicodemus went to Jesus at night (John 3:1-5). In our neighborhood, we call that a visit on the "down low." He didn't want his friends to see and his elevated place in society to be threatened. Jesus quickly put him on his heels with the declaration that though he was the great teacher of Israel, unless he experienced Christian conversion he would not see the kingdom of God. Very few probably spoke to Nicodemus in such a challenging manner. His response to Jesus was not asking *why* he needed to convert. His question was "how" (John 3:4).

Jesus trained the 72 into how process conversion works. They needed to understand conversion and master the fundamentals if they were to prove faithful and fruitful under the crushing pressure.

CHAPTER THEME: Jesus trains the 72 in how God brings people to faith.

CORE TEXT: Exegesis of Luke 10:21-24

> *In that same hour he rejoiced in the Holy Spirit and said, "I thank you, Father, Lord of heaven and earth, that you have hidden these things from the wise and understanding and revealed them to little children; yes, Father, for such was your gracious will. All things have been handed over to me by my Father, and no one knows who the Son is except the Father, or who the Father is except the Son and anyone to whom the Son chooses to reveal him."*
>
> *Then turning to the disciples he said privately, "Blessed are the eyes that see what you see! For I tell you that many prophets and kings desired to see what you see, and did not see it, and to hear what you hear, and didn't hear it."*

These verses are a crucial theological centerpiece of the overall equipping and training of the 72. As I worked through this section, I asked myself, "How would our training be different if these verses were not present?" I believe that this section provides a bookend to the opening verses of the chapter. Jesus begins with a call to pray to the Lord of the harvest. The section ends with Jesus peeling back the mysterious veil to instruct us of the Father's good work in conversion. The disciples pray; the Father acts. The beginning and the end of the 72 training are spiritual as profound movement and transformation are happening in the next dimension.

The major training element that these four verses provide is that God the Father and Jesus the Son both choose those who will come to faith. When you and I came to faith, while it was our human experience of choice, verse 21 teaches us that in the spiritual realm, God the Father graciously willed our conversions. The second half of the same verse goes on to teach us that because of God's gracious will, the Son has full authority to reveal himself to anyone whom he chooses.

While this might not first be interpreted as "stop the presses (or blog post)" news, it is worth noting that Jesus and the Father have

Figure 4.1. The conversion process

a plan. Christian conversion is not haphazard, random, or by chance. God has a plan, and it is our calling to understand Christian conversion by observing patterns and trends, and by testing our theories.

THE TECHNICAL THEORY OF PROCESS CONVERSION

The great missionary to India, E. Stanley Jones, reminds us of the need to articulate clearly the centrality of the new birth in our evangelism theory and practice: "Jesus drew a line down through all these distinctions and divided humanity into just two classes—the unconverted and the converted, the once born and the twice born. All of humanity lives on one side or the other of that line."[1]

Being a good person is not enough. Loving and meeting practical needs of those in pain, while important, are not enough. The call of the 72 is to be a part of the faith and conversion process that will result in the salvation of those we love. The goal is new birth, faith, and seeing what kings and prophets never saw: the mission field of the church becoming the mission force of the church. We must remember that the 72 themselves started on the unconverted line of humanity and by Luke 10 were the sent ones living out and proclaiming the message of salvation.

In order to understand conversion, I conducted a survey to discover evangelism leadership principles in the Evangelical Covenant Church, a smaller denomination that has been called "the denomination that fights above its weight class." We currently have 925 churches and a hundred pastors who shared in my research project. Mining from their ministry experiences, they answered the following question: "How do people become Christian in a normal and natural way in your context?" The study stressed biblical conversion, not merely a decision that made some mythical scorecard but had no transformative impact.[2]

There are indeed many ways in which the Holy Spirit brings people to saving faith, but I'm also acutely aware that pastors and lay leaders alike need a framework in order to train their people into practical evangelism. A communal concept must be promoted to ministry teams so contextualization may occur. I am confident that this framework is rooted in enough common data that it might bear fruit in your ministry context.

Four central elements rose to the top of the research. It became clear that there was a pattern of conversion to be considered. (1) The conversion pastors and ministry leaders reported followed an inversion of the modern process of conversion. (2) Almost all of the converts made it a point to note that a Christian was praying for them during their season of personal awakening to faith. (3) Genuine friendships where a Christian helped the non-Christian move from the secular to the sacred occurred across the board. (4) Courageous preachers and personal evangelists gave the unbeliever an invitation to cross over into the twice-born side of humanity. To represent this part of the research project, we created a diagram of the process of conversion.

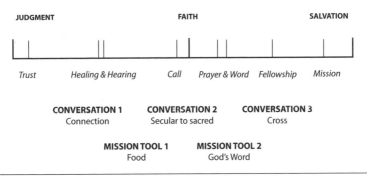

Figure 4.2. Conversion process timeline

Analysis of the research also led our ministry team to construct a linear timeline (figure 4.2). I use this tool almost daily as I lead our local church, FOL, to gauge process conversion and to chart growth to mature discipleship. I also believe it's a perspective on the process of conversion that helps us know exactly what we're called to do and when we're called to do it.

When we meet up with non-Christians, the first question that must be asked is "How far away is he from the kingdom of God?" Jesus taught the 72 to tell the people that the kingdom of God was near. The concept of space, journey, and a point in time is important enough to Jesus that he would train his evangelists to ask this question. This is where our relationships as the 72 always begin.

Is the new person we have befriended someone with a strong church background, studied the Bible as a youth, trusts Christians, but recently fell into sin or major transition and is no longer living by faith? Maybe your friend is a former member of a church but is disillusioned because their pastor stole the building fund, left his wife, and ran off with the church secretary, who happened to be their cousin. These are both true stories from people that I heard as I built trust with them. Every person you meet has a story. It's our job to know where we're starting. On the outside, both people look the same when you're sharing a meal together. But when you get below the surface, ask a few questions, and truly listen to what they say, I believe you can gather enough data that you can have an accurate read on how far away they are from the kingdom of God.

FOUR, THREE, TWO, ONE

The conversion process timeline features four benchmark events that all converts experience. The normal and natural path of conversion begins with trust. Unless there is direct intervention from the Holy Trinity or a supernatural angelic being, trusting a Christian is the essential starting point. Fruitful evangelists Doug Schaupp and Don Everts offer the following comments on trust in the context of evangelism outreach: "Trust is always a gift of the heart. Trust between two people is so valuable and precious that is should never be taken for granted."[3]

We must also be proactive in establishing trust with non-Christian friends if they are to embark on a life of trusting Jesus. Once trust is established, the mature evangelist will lead the non-Christian into the benchmarks of healing, hearing, and committing to the gospel unimpeded. There will be challenges, twists, and turns, but for the most part, building trust and getting others acquainted with Jesus is the hardest part of the conversion process. Chapters five, six, and seven will provide insights and practical skills you can build upon.

Again, it's absolutely imperative that we diagnose correctly if our friends are to trust Christians and the church. If they live in a place of trust, the conversion process may be quick; but if the church or other Christians have hurt them, the evangelism timeline must be extended because of a deficit of trust. I contend that many of the conflicts, broken relationships, and negative experiences we have in evangelism are because we haven't done the hard work of diagnosing the starting points of our friends.

Three conversations are necessary to help our non-Christian friends navigate the process conversion timeline. It's the rare convert who works her way through to the other side of the boundary without human aid. Conversion Conversation 1 is called "Initial Investigation." This is the conversation where the 72 evangelist asks about their spiritual background, listens with all his ears, mind, and heart, and comes up with an initial diagnosis of where they are on the conversion process timeline.

Conversion Conversation 2 is "Secular to Sacred." Through an invitation to participate in prayer, God's Word, and fellowship with Christians, the nature of the friendship changes to include Jesus and the gospel.

The final spiritual heart-to-heart is Conversion Conversation 3: "Curiosity to Cross." Once the new convert has learned the story of the gospel, experienced the transformative power of the Word, and begun to build friendships with mature Christians in the local church, she is ready for the commitment conversation. Her faith is not active until she drops her nets and picks up her cross. Whether public or private, every person who experiences the new birth needs a call to commit to Jesus and the way of the cross.

The Lord sends the 72 into the harvest with two mission tools to win the lost: food and the Word of God. In the first stage of building trust and inviting our friends into God's Word, food is a great evangelistic weapon to genuinely enjoy our friends, to bond, and to learn where they are on the process conversion timeline (Luke 10:7). In the kingdom of God, faith comes through hearing the gospel, the Word of God. The 72 were instructed to teach their friends that "the kingdom of God has come near" (Luke 10:11). I believe that is Luke's manner of summarizing the verbal proclamation ministry of the 72. I don't believe the 72 said that exact phrase exclusively but used it as a summary of the teaching ministry they delivered to those they ministered to.

THREE EVANGELISM TRENDS

The 72 were sent into actual towns, villages, and cities to reach people on the margins. Jesus told them that he was sending them where he himself was planning to go. Knowing that Jesus follows his witnesses should change our understanding of evangelism. "Whoever we give our witness to, and under whatever circumstances we deliver our testimony, it is enough for Jesus."[4] The people in those areas were real people in real cultures with real ways of doing life together. When Jesus trained the 72, he made sure that they would be strong, bold, and firm. While honoring the culture, they were to take full advantage of "gospel openings" in the hearts, minds, souls, and bodies of unbelievers. We would do well to step back for perspective, ask God to help us work smarter, and ask ourselves what we're learning about non-Christians and how they are processing life.

I agree with Dave Olson that there are three dominant trends at work in current culture that we as the 72 must embrace in order to be effective in evangelism. He wrote,

> The American Church must engage with these three critical transitions: Our world used to be Christian, but it is now becoming post-Christian. Our world used to be modern, but it is now becoming post-modern. Our world used to be mono-ethnic, but it is now becoming multiethnic. In many states and metropolitan areas, these transitions are occurring rapidly.[5]

PERSONAL TRUTH IS TRENDING

There are many characteristics ascribed to postmoderns, millennials, and the younger generations today. They are innovative, creative, socially minded, and eager to heal the social ills that plague planet Earth. They are tech savvy, communal, well traveled, and eager to find the best food in any city with their smartphone in a matter of seconds.

But they also have been called flighty. The fear of missing out leads them occasionally to listen carefully to the wanderlust that is so prevalent in their generation, calling them first to experience the greener grass in another city, rather than working on watering their own lawn. The average length of job service for millennials is just below two years. I believe that the evangelism vision must stay young and reach the next generation if we have any hope of a fresh expression in their own language. I have also heard from many older Christians that they are ready to give up because young people have "given up truth." I don't believe the evidence bears out this claim. Millennials haven't rejected truth, but they process truth through the filter of personal experience.

How often have you heard the phrase "That may be true for you, but not for me"? Many Christians find that those words are the deal breaker of any evangelistic conversation. Personally, when I hear those words, my heart begins to race a little, and I get excited because we are beginning to get to the good stuff. I've found that phrase to be a wonderful opening to take the conversation of experiencing God for themselves deeper. At no other time in human history have worldviews been so dependent on personal experience. If you help people participate in and enjoy an experience, they will process it as truth.

Doug Schaupp and Don Everts define some of the key characteristics of postmodern generations: "We are more experiential than propositional in our connection to truth. We are more communal than individualistic. We value authenticity over theory. We understand struggle more than naive certainty. We are in process, and we will be different in ten or twenty years."[6] How will the evangelism in our generation reflect the values of postmoderns and millennials? If the gospel is not good news to them, we must consider our language and methods.

A few years back, I was the speaker for a series of evangelistic outreaches at the University of Southern California. For the first night, I was pleased at the good work of outreach. The Christian Trojans brought their friends and filled the auditorium. I spoke about God, destiny, and the practical steps we must take to understand and pursue God's plan for our lives. To bring it all home, I used Dallas Willard as the prime example of why we need a mentor. Willard, a giant in the Christian faith, was also a professor of philosophy at the secular university. I thought holding him out as the example would be good news to the hearer.

I invited the skeptics and seekers to fill out a card and meet with me for coffee the next day so I could be a "Dallas Willard" in their lives. I expected twenty to thirty responses. The numbers were disappointing. Exactly zero students signed up to meet with me.

The next evening was a carbon copy of the previous night with the same level of promotion, a packed auditorium, and an evangelistic sermon. On the second night, I changed the ending. Instead of using Willard as an example for seeking mentoring, I used the voice of Yoda from the Star Wars movies. I said, "Spiritual mentor you need," but I expected very few responses. Surprisingly, over twenty students signed up for a personal meeting. The students hadn't changed overnight, but my content had.

If Jesus were training the 72 today, I believe he would teach them to speak in personal truths first, followed by propositional truths, so that young people hear the message of Jesus as good news. To be a powerful member of the 72, we must embrace how younger people process truth.

BIBLICAL ILLITERACY IS TRENDING

America is becoming more and more post-Christian. Again Olson laments that "the Church must discover what century they are living in."[7] He believes that a tipping point occurred at the millennial shift, which altered the relationship between American culture and the church, forever changing how the two relate to each other.[8] In the old Christian world, pastors, churches, and individual believers operated as the majority in society. It was as though church growth and evangelism were built into the system. To start an "outreach Bible study," all you had to do was put a sign on the church door, and twenty people would show up because it was the right thing to do. This is the model that attracts lost sons and daughters who have a strong Christian foundation; if someone builds it, they will come.

With outreach being so easy, much of the energy of a church was given to the "insiders" for important matters such as membership and discipleship. But with the new generation emerging, the landscape has changed dramatically. They want to pursue Jesus and the gospel differently from their parents, and they critique the "boomer model" of Christian leadership. Cities are flooded with these new faces, many having little to no church background. Put these all together with the number of churches that do little to reach non-Christians in their community, and it's no wonder conversion numbers are plummeting. For most American churches, a transition to defining church membership as mission is a great challenge. The disappearance of Christendom has produced a sense of grief and loss.[9]

Despite these trends, I believe that the Bible itself is an important tool for evangelism. I'm continually amazed at how many people from many different walks of life are genuinely curious and open to learning about the Bible. They haven't experienced church, and they are biblically illiterate. They would be hard-pressed to name one or two of the sixty-six books, letters, and historical accounts in the Bible. What are the odds they can name two central characters from the Old and New Testament (apart from Jesus, Adam and Eve, and the sneaky snake in the garden)? And yet I find in almost all the unbelievers I meet and talk to on a spiritual level a profound curiosity, "bigger than me" respect, and in some cases even reverence for the Word.

Where does this internal and external belief that the Bible is at some level at least important come from? Darrell Johnson believes it's part of our hard wiring as humans designed by the living God. "The fundamental issue facing humanity is whom will I worship?" he says. "Fish swim. Birds fly. Humans worship. Someone has said that we human beings are incurably religious, meaning we can't but worship someone or something. Who will it be?"[10] Since we are wired for worship, of course there will be a predisposition to the very source of our worship.

Many unbelievers know God and the Bible are important without articulating that they know. Seeing the world as biblically illiterate but open to learning should affect our view. How will the evangelism of the modern-day 72 reflect the issues of our post-Christian world?

I recently taught a devotional lesson to secular, urban high school students. As we spoke about sexuality and God's call to celibacy until heterosexual marriage as the definition of faithfulness, one student asked, "Is not having sex really a part of the ten amendments?"

Another person visited our church and told me he was beginning to read the Bible. He needed wisdom, and a friend had told him to read Proverbs. With an entirely genuine heart and zeal to learn, he asked, "Pastor, is there a book about amateur verbs too?"

A lack of biblical knowledge offers the 72 an amazing opportunity. The world is drawn to this mysterious collection of sixty-six books that our Father in heaven has authored. And they are thirsty for the spiritual experience that comes from the living Word. If Jesus were training the 72 today, I believe he would teach his followers to teach the Word and to speak about the One who was revealed in the Bible. There is great power available to the 72 as we deliver God's Word to unbelievers.

MULTIETHNICITY IS TRENDING

The third trend Olson highlights is America's transition from monoethnic to multiethnic. In the old world, Christian pastors and witnesses only had to understand their cultures. Now, massive population shift is a global reality, especially in the emergence of large, multiethnic cities.[11] For the past fifty years, God has been bringing all the nations of the world into the big cities of the world.

For millennials today, the vast majority of their lives has been multiethnic. In the public schools of our nations megacities, hundreds of languages are spoken. Young people today are wired and connected in such a way that they're gaming in Seattle with friends they have never met in Beijing. Their music heroes are named Jackson, Shakur, and Jay Z. Their sports heroes are named Jordan, Bryant, and Messi. Their forty-fourth president was a biracial African American man from Hawaii. On their phones, they receive real-time updates about protests in Hong Kong, the civil war in Syria, and terror threats in Europe, while they call for their Uber driver, who will most likely be a person from another culture. When it comes to church, however, it's as though they've entered a time warp and returned to the simple streets of 1950s homogenous America.

The world is shrinking and getting more multiethnic by the moment. I remember meeting a Kuwaiti man at a tennis tournament. He was very wealthy and said that he spent eight weeks a year flying to the Australian Open, French Open, Wimbledon, and the US Open to watch Roger Federer. I politely smiled while trying to hide the covetousness that was exploding in my heart. He asked me where I was from. I told him Long Beach, California. Without skipping a beat, this middle-aged man from Kuwait raised his hand like a rapper, waved it side to side, and proudly exclaimed, "Snoooooop Doggggg!" I was amused and intrigued by Long Beach hip-hop's global impact reaching all the way to Kuwait.

In their groundbreaking work, *Divided by Faith*, authors Emerson and Smith define a racially mixed congregation as "one in which the dominant culture of the group is less than 80 percent or more of the congregation." Personally I believe this to be a very lenient and generous definition of a multiethnic church. And yet, at the time of the research, the number of racially mixed churches in the United State was just under 8 percent of the over three hundred thousand evangelical, mainline, and Catholic churches.

While many churches promote themselves as a multiethnic church family online because that is the popular thing to do, finding churches that actually live into this vision is very hard. I like to joke that when searching for the multiethnic and multiclass church that Jesus describes in Luke 4, you have a better shot at finding Bigfoot roaming the snowy Alaskan forests. Our future is multiethnic because that's millenials' experience in almost every domain of their lives. But is the church agile enough to adapt? The comedian Chris Rock struck a chord for us when he said, "You know the world is changing when the best rapper is white and the best golfer is black." And I would add that one of the decade's most sensational NBA stars is Asian American.

If Jesus were training the 72 today, I believe he would teach them to engage in authentic crosscultural evangelistic friendships. Crosscultural personal evangelism is one of the most important ministry skills the next generation of Christians will need to be competent in. My friend Soong-Chan Rah wrote, "In the next evangelicalism, the second generation with their unique ethos and strength along with those in our churches who have crosscultural, liminal experiences, will be the ones best equipped to face the next stage of the church."[12] There is great power in learning as the 72 prepare for an even more multiethnic future.

TOKYO EVANGELISM INSIGHTS

I've found the ministry of Takeshi Takazawa, one of my church-planting colleagues in Tokyo, Japan, most helpful in illuminating the disparity between modern and postmodern conversion. I try to observe what the Holy Spirit is doing and on a human level "what is working" in the most challenging ministry regions, because those values and principles will likely transfer into easier contexts. Evangelism and conversion that leads to discipleship in Tokyo is hard.

Takazawa is a church planter and mission leader in Tokyo. He makes the astute observation that converts have always experienced at least three transformations within Christian conversion: church, truth, and Christian community.[13] The modernist is converted by entering through the door of church, embracing the truth as laid out in the proclamation of the gospel, and then building friendships within the relational structure as offered by the church. The postmodern conversion process, however, is inverted. Most of the converts he has seen in Asia come to faith through friendships, experiencing the truths of the kingdom in relationship with Christian friends, and then finally enter officially into the church. Takazawa argues that postmoderns who are at the point of conversion have already internalized the story of Jesus and the myriad benefits that come with faith, but they do not yet know what they believe.

"I BELIEVE. PLEASE TELL ME WHAT I BELIEVE"

A few years ago, I came across a testimony that perfectly captures our working theory of process conversion. I was teaching the New Testament Mission course at Pacific Rim Christian University in Honolulu, Hawaii. I asked the class to challenge this theory of how people around the globe are converting today. Every student who had recently come to faith affirmed that this was their testimony of how they had converted.

Sayako, one of the students in the course, was from a church plant in Yokohama, a city one hour west of Tokyo. She told the story of a friend who recently came to faith. Many of the believers in her small group were friends with the young woman and prayed for her conversion. The Lord particularly brought her to mind, and they began to pray earnestly that God would send workers to her. They noticed that she began to hunger for God and attended their weekly Bible studies. Her personal experiences within the Bible study were very energizing and life giving, so she began to attend Sunday worship services. She went on to become a regular attender of the church for two months.

At one of the Sunday services, as the Word went out, she was deeply convicted of her sin and her need for faith in Christ. The Holy Spirit had come upon her, and she wanted to become a woman of faith and begin her new life as a disciple of Christ. After the service, she went up to stand beside the pastor. He was so busy greeting guests and praying for people, he didn't greet her. Over the course of three straight Sundays, though she went up and stood near the pastor, they never connected. On the fourth Sunday, she didn't know what to say, but she knew she had to say something. So again, she went and stood by the pastor.

Like the living God parted the Red Sea, that Sunday, the people moved out, and she was able to reach the pastor. She inserted herself into the line, met the pastor, and blurted out, "I have seen this community and heard from God in the Bible. I am ready. I believe! I believe!" The pastor joyfully received this testimony from the woman and was ready to pray for her. Before he could speak his first words to her, the woman said, "I believe. But could you please tell me what I believe?"

THE 72 MINISTRY COUNTDOWN

Jesus taught the 72 how conversion works. They needed to master the process so they would be effective even under crushing pressure. For the next three chapters, we'll focus on the primary ministry tasks the 72 accomplished over and over and over to win the lost.

The 72 led their friends into four timeline benchmarks, sat down for three boundary conversations, used two mission tools, and helped their friends across one line of faith.

With the power of the Holy Spirit, it's as easy as four, three, two, one.

EARNEST AND
POWERFUL PRAYERS

If you are called to lead a ministry, you
are called to pray for that ministry.

DR. J. ROBERT CLINTON

THE EVANGELISM TRAINING MEETING

I wonder what the 72 expected when they arrived for their training event with Jesus. Luke gives us no visual details of the gathering, which I think might help us explore the setting with a sanctified imagination. While the Lord evangelized, taught, and even cooked breakfasts on the beautiful shores of Galilee, prayer and training events were often held inside. In the Gospels, he ministered publicly but then retreated to debrief and explain ministry concepts to his disciples. The early church gathered in the home of John Mark's mother. I wonder if that was built on the tradition of Jesus meeting with his disciples in the home of Peter's mother-in-law (Mark 1:29). The first Gospel tells us that the whole city was gathered inside and around the door. It could easily have accommodated seventy-two disciples.

I envision Peter, James, John, and the rest of the Twelve serving as greeters, welcoming the 72 to their training event. With food and drink such a central part of Jesus' ministry in Luke's Gospel, I bet the meeting had amazing hummus and Mediterranean juices. The energy must have been palpable. The 72 had probably been very curious about who else would be there. When they saw friends from public teaching times, they likely hugged or shook hands.

When Jesus came into the room, I imagine all eyes were fixed on him and all mouths quieted. As a wonderful rabbi and a leader of such hospitality, I'm certain he introduced his twelve disciples first, allowed the 72 to break the ice together, and then introduced himself in a self-deprecating and humble manner. When Jesus, the teaching rabbi, finally sat to address the students, the first item on his agenda was prayer. I wish we had the chance to learn firsthand from Jesus!

Imagine all the evangelism knowledge Jesus desired to pass on to his faithful disciples. Yes, they would need to know about culture, but he didn't start with culture. They would go out and perform miraculous deeds of healing and deliverance to authenticate the gospel message, but he didn't start with power. I'm sure they all felt a great need for input on communication, knowing exactly what to say and what not to say. But Jesus didn't start with communication. So much of life in the first-century Mediterranean culture revolved around food and fellowship. But Jesus didn't start a teaching on the power of ministering with food or of having followup structures in place.

Nope. He didn't begin with ministry strategy. And he didn't say a thing about how his team of first-timers would handle the bitter sting of rejection. That would come later. Many training issues legitimately could have been number one on the meeting agenda—but weren't.

Jesus started with prayer.

CHAPTER THEME: The ministry of the 72 is supernatural so Jesus instructs them how to pray for their ministry.

CORE TEXT: Luke 10:1-2

After this the Lord appointed seventy-two others and sent them on ahead of him, two by two, into every town and place where he himself was about to go. And he said to them, "The harvest is plentiful, but the laborers are few. Therefore pray earnestly to the Lord of the harvest to send out laborers into his harvest."

The first training component is very clear. The development and deployment of kingdom workers involves faith and prayer. This teaching is the only moment in all of the Scripture when Jesus taught exactly what to pray for and exactly how to pray for it. What are we to pray for? We are to pray for more kingdom workers. And in what manner are we to engage in prayer? We are to pray earnestly. The word *earnest* means to operate with great focus and great feeling. Our prayers to the Lord of the harvest are to be sober, serious, passionate, and full of sincere depth. When we pray in this way, we aren't just saying words; we feel like we are making history.

FOL ANTIOCH

In 2013, our church started a new organization called Fountain of Life Antioch, the church-planting wing of our ten-year-old church plant. The purpose of the organization is to mentor and resource church planters in the inner cities of America and underevangelized megacities of Asia.

I invested two years studying the book of Acts as a core-book Bible study. I learned that Paul of Tarsus, the great church planter, was blessed with the spiritual gift of apostleship. An apostle has five primary functions: (1) start new churches and supporting ministries; (2) develop leaders; (3) fight heresy; (4) fund the new ministries; and (5) pray for new and old works. When we study Paul's ministry, we see he was the first to break down spiritual walls to plant new churches. As he matured, his model of developing younger church planters grew as he equipped and resourced them for their own church planting. FOL Antioch mentors current and future church planters into those five apostolic tasks.

Our first international church plant was launched in Hong Kong. I was invited by the Mission Covenant Church of Hong Kong to speak to the mission leaders in the denomination at their annual pastors' gathering. The entire auditorium of ministry leaders from Hong Kong and Mainland China was very open and eager to receive God's Word. I preached for three days from the book of Acts on the theme "How the Church Began."

Our team quickly bonded with the national leaders as we enjoyed community, fellowship, and absolutely amazing Hong Kong cuisine. We even discovered that we shared common mission friends. (Los Angeles and other West Coast megacities function as extensions of Asia, prompting missiologist Ray Bakke to affectionately refer to Vancouver as "Hong-couver.")

At the end of the conference, Simon and Millie Yeung and Reverend Stephen Tam shared that their denomination had a vision to plant eight new churches by 2020. They said that during the conference, they had been praying, and they asked us to consider if we were receiving a "Macedonian call" to minister in Hong Kong. They also asked that we help them plant the new churches. Our ministry team prayed about it, and we quickly discerned that the Lord had opened a great door for us.

In the fall of 2016, we visited the site for our third church plant in Hong Kong in the Sham Shui Po district of Kowloon. This area is the poorest in Hong Kong. Many people there are recent immigrants from Mainland China who live with their families in 236-square-foot apartments provided by the government. The

Lord has raised up a gifted businessman, Kevin Yoong, to faithfully and generously provide venues for the new churches through a chain of Taiwan-based restaurants called Tino's Pizza. It's a risky business model to place a restaurant in the economically depressed area of Sham Shui Po, but for the sake of building a church, providing community, and reaching the lost in Hong Kong, the contracts have been signed. Kevin has made a commitment in faith to love God—not his profit margins.

EARNEST PRAYERS IN HONG KONG

On our last trip, we visited where this third church will be launched. The previous owners had just cleared out, and it was an empty warehouse right on the main thoroughfare. With the Mission Covenant Church leaders, we gathered in a circle and prayed earnestly to the Lord of the harvest. When Reverend Tam began to pray in his native Cantonese, it was as though my soul were filling with fire. His words of praise, blessing, and love exploded through the roof. He thanked God for new church plants, all of the new leaders God was calling and training, his amazing provision, and the joy of the gospel. As he began to pray that God would send kingdom workers to the good people of Sham Shui Po, my heart soared. I thanked God for letting me be a part of his great plans.

A recent convert to the Hong Kong church then began to pray. On the metro train ride over, he had shared how God had delivered him from a life of excess, alcohol, and drug abuse through the evangelism ministry of Reverend Tam. He was an artist and photographer who hoped to turn his talents into a ministry. There's something so refreshing and honest about the prayers of the new believers.

I didn't understand what he said, because every word he prayed was in Cantonese, but I felt what he said. Because I knew his conversion story and what God had done to make him a man of faith,

I was blown away by his passion, his belief that God rescues sinners, and the power behind his prayers.

And I was not the only one. The main garage-style doors to the warehouse were open, and many Hong Kong residents stopped and ducked in from the overcrowded and hectic street to see what was going on. The onlookers seemed to be drawn by his passion, by the spiritual heat. Power was moving in the atmosphere. One woman walked in and watched us pray for close to ten minutes. When we had concluded our prayers, one of the evangelists on our team went to her. I trust that the Lord of the harvest is at work in her life.

When we pray for evangelism, our default prayer content and style is often focused on a seemingly unthinkable task, and in desperation we pray for God to somehow make the impossible possible. I find myself praying that people will be "open to the gospel," because sadly my default is that people aren't open to the gospel. When we walk into a Starbucks and see fifty people, how many of us believe that twenty are open to the gospel? Do we consider that some of the people there are only one conversation, a Bible study, or an answered prayer away from beginning their faith relationship with Jesus? We imagine a closed door, expecting that everyone we talk to will say, "No thank you," or worse if we talk about Jesus, unless we experience a renewal of our minds. We pray as though there has been no witness in the lives of our friends. I believe we are far too focused on people being "open."

It's clear that Jesus didn't feel the need to train the 72 in praying for openness in those who would hear the message. Yes, there will be rejection, but there will be reception as well.

THE BIGGEST PROBLEM IN THE NEW TESTAMENT

How many of us believe that "the harvest is plentiful"? We look with our unaided eyes and see so many people going through the motions of life, pushing through the same routines, trying to live good lives. The kingdom of God is neither a priority nor a reality to those whom Jesus says are ripe for harvest. His perspective and vision are greater than that of the 72. I wonder if the original 72 rolled their eyes a bit and whispered to their neighbors, "What harvest is he talking about?" His eyes are very different, because he sees the spiritual dimension.

Jesus boldly trained and declared that some people are already open. I wonder what the tone in his voice was when he taught his friends that the harvest really is ripe. Fruit is present, full, and falling off the trees. It's absolutely great in quality and quantity. I think of the amazing image in Numbers 13, when Joshua and Caleb arrived back from the Promised Land carrying branches that bent under the weight of the fruit. So the problem is not a lack of fruit. The Holy Spirit has already been at work, sometimes for decades and decades, preparing unbelievers to the point that they can be described as ripe fruit. They are juicy, colorful, and waiting to be picked.

But there aren't enough people to pick the fruit. We might believe and live as though the problem is that people aren't open to the gospel. But the real problem is the labor force. The product of the gospel is incredible, and the demand for the gospel is overwhelming; unfortunately, the distribution channels are very limited for delivering the gospel to sinners on whom God is at work to redeem.

What is the biggest problem in the New Testament? Is it sin? I think not. We can all affirm that sin, with all of its insidious, destructive, and demonic ways, causes ruin throughout our world on a daily basis. But theologically Jesus has taken care of sin. He has made the perfect one-time offering to the living God. John's Gospel reminds us that it is indeed finished.

Is the biggest problem in the New Testament broken relationships? Unreconciled relationships, estrangement, unforgiveness, and bitterness may be present and powerful in our lives. As Paul teaches in Ephesians 2, Jesus in his flesh has broken down the dividing wall of hostility (Ephesians 2:14). Is the biggest problem in the New Testament financial greed and injustice? Paul taught that the love of money is the root of all evil (1 Timothy 6:10). As we study our world today, the gap between rich and poor has never been greater, but God is powerfully at work to lift the low and bring down the proud, sending the rich away empty-handed. Luke instructed that God's plan is doing just fine, and having faith means finding ourselves on the right side of history.

No, the greatest problem in the New Testament is a labor distribution issue. It's as though doctors, scientists, and the smartest people in the global medical community have finally broken through with a cure for cancer. The medicine has been tested and proven, and the results are a clean bill of health for all infected. They have even figured out how to mass-produce the cure. But no one is there to deliver the message.

The great English preacher G. Campbell Morgan reminds us that Jesus, the wise leader, called on the 72 as his distribution plan: "That mission was something quite new in the method of Jesus. It was a planned campaign. In the first three years of His ministry, there seems to have been an absence of what we should call organization. Here, on the contrary, is the account of a carefully organized work."[1]

So there's enough medicine for every single person on planet Earth who is sick. But there aren't enough people who believe in the medicine to devote their lives to getting it to those who need it. The biggest problem in the New Testament is there are simply not enough workers for the plentiful harvest. This is why, on that amazing day in Capernaum, Jesus trained the 72 to be part of his distribution mission. And this is why Jesus, through the Holy Spirit, is doing the exact same thing today.

In teaching the 72 to pray this way, Jesus instills a mind-set of sovereign hope. To be effective, like the 72, we have to believe that God is already at work. Evangelism is not going into newly formed relationships doing all we can to create a hunger for God. Evangelism is becoming flesh in a situation where God is already at work. The hard work has already been done.

As we pray like this, at least two spiritual developments will occur. The first is that God will use our prayers to increase our sensitivity to the Spirit and boldness in the gospel. Over and over again, I have seen those who pray for more workers become the answer to their own prayers. As you pray for more kingdom workers, God will help you become a kingdom worker. And you're likely to be sent to those you are praying for.

The second development is that we become more sensitive to where God is working. As we consider who God has strategically put into our lives, and as we pray with great zeal for the Lord of the harvest to send workers, we will be quicker to take notice of his work in their lives. Without prayer, we can't see spiritual realities that are present but often invisible. Without prayer, we won't be led to ask question that help us see that the person is ripe fruit waiting to be gathered. And without prayer, we walk around our cities with our heads down instead of walking with our chins up, expectant and eager to meet whomever God has prepared for us.

I've seen great joy in the 72 who pray this way. And there's no greater joy than seeing the Holy Spirit work through the consistent and passionate prayers for the people in our lives. There is no greater hope than believing that our churches and our cities are mission fields that are ripe for harvest. Do we live as though we might meet the next great convert to Christianity right around the corner?

Because the Lord of the harvest was at work long before the 72 received the summons to their day of training, hope is our reality.

WHO WE PRAY TO

Prayer is a great mystery. While we pray earnestly, we must remember that prayer works not because of how we pray, but because of who we pray to. It's an amazing thought that God invites us into the process of transformation through prayer. It's incredible that the living God will use our very words to affect the eternal outcomes of our friends.

Darrell Johnson, in his book on the Lord's Prayer, *57 Words That Change the World*, highlights what Blaise Pascal calls "the dignity of causality." God takes us and our prayers very seriously. It's no accident that we're invited to pray and literally change the outcomes in our world and in the world to come. We have amazing power in every conversation with God, in ever plea for broken sinners, and in every tear of brokenness and despair. Somehow and in some dimension, God receives the prayers of the saints and uses them as ingredients to bring people from the kingdom of darkness into the kingdom of light.

I believe that the efficacy and scope of our prayers are a great barometer for our knowledge of the character of the Father. If we believe that he is present, generous, and delighted to answer prayer, we ask for much. If we believe he's stingy, tightfisted, and distant, why bother going before him on our knees? Our prayer journals are faithful accounts of how well we understand the character of the Father.

DINNER WITH VIN SCULLY

Growing up, I was a massive fan of the Los Angeles Dodgers. My best friend's mother, Dolores Buonauro, served for over three decades as the secretary for the Dodgers' front office. When Fred

Claire, the former general manager of the Dodgers, resigned after being caught in the tectonic plates of the controversial purchase of the Dodgers by FOX, he said that what he would miss most about his job was saying good night to Dolores.

Throughout high school, my friends and I visited at least one game each home stand and spent most summer nights at Dodger Stadium. And as any Dodgers fan can tell you, the biggest, brightest, and longest-shining star in the organization is Vin Scully. I remember hearing Vin's mellifluous voice as a five-year-old watching the games on television and listening on the radio. Four decades later, at the time of this writing, he's still going strong at the age of eighty-eight. I know I'm not alone when I say he became like a family member to me.

In my philosophy class during my first year at the local community college, our instructor was a very cool surfer who lived out a very laid-back philosophy. As he passed out the semester syllabus, he told us the content of our term paper: "Your assignment is to interview any living philosopher." Someone in the class asked what that meant. He replied, "Interview any living person that lives by a philosophy." Immediately, I knew I had to interview Vin Scully.

Being a college student prone to procrastination, as the term was winding down, I went home and wrote what I thought was a very eloquent letter to him. I included our very one-sided history together and his impact on my life, stressing how much I enjoyed Shakespeare quotes during long at-bats. I ended the letter with a request for an interview so that I might do well in my philosophy class. The letter was addressed, sealed, and sent. And I had great confidence that I would be interviewing Vin Scully.

But something funny happened on the way to arranging the meeting. I received a written reply from Vin, declining the interview. I was crushed. I was also anxious because the deadline for my term paper was just around the corner. But on a deeper level, I was deeply disappointed because I had my heart set on interviewing him.

I thought, *Vin wouldn't turn me down. I need to ask again.*

So I called Mrs. Buonauro and met her at Dodger Stadium. It was a Thursday night game, and the Dodgers had a weekend home stand with the Cincinnati Reds. Dolores provided me great assistance with Vin's postgame schedule and some insider tips on how I might get a face-to-face connection with him. If it sounds like I was stalking Vin Scully, it's because I was. But I didn't care. I had to hear from his mouth that he didn't want to meet with me.

About an hour after the game, he emerged from the press box and got onto the Club Level elevator. I got on too. There was a woman on the elevator who chatted with Vin about a meal she and her husband shared with him back in the day in St. Louis. As he replied to her comments, I couldn't believe that I was standing next to that voice. I pinched myself as I realized I was sharing the elevator with one of my heroes. As the doors opened, the woman and Vin said good-bye, and he began to walk toward his car in the empty upper-level parking lot.

I was a few feet behind him when I called out, "Mr. Scully."

He casually turned around to greet me with a warm smile. I tried to act like I had been there before, but I ended up blurting out in a language that I think resembled English, "I'm John Teter, and I wrote you and requested an interview for my philosophy term paper."

Mr. Scully tilted his head to the side a bit and kindly said, "I'm sorry. I get quite a bit of mail. I have a publicist and unfortunately, because of my travel schedule, he has to decline almost all of the requests."

I nodded, shook my head in acknowledgment, and prepared to turn to walk back toward the elevator. But Vin said, "John, what can I do for you?" I quickly regurgitated almost verbatim what I had written in the letter. He was a very patient listener. I asked him for an interview then waited for a few moments that seemed to me like nine innings.

He looked me in the eye and asked, "Do you have tickets for tomorrow night's game?"

I answered, "Yes, I have a ticket through Dolores Buonauro."

He said, "Very good. Just spell your name out for me, and I'll leave it at the press box door. Let's have dinner tomorrow evening during my third-inning break."

My face lit up, and my heart soared. "Thanks so much, Mr. Scully. I will see you tomorrow night."

The next night, we arrived for the game very early to watch batting practice. I was so nervous. The game began, and the first inning went quickly. My hands started sweating as the second inning began. Soon I was minutes away from having dinner with Vin Scully. Once the final out of the second inning was recorded, I calmly rose from my seat. I looked at my friends, and as if I had been in that situation a thousand times before, I looked at my watch and nonchalantly mentioned, "Well, it looks like it's time to go to the press box and have dinner with Vin Scully." They shook their heads in disbelief.

I don't remember if my feet hit the ground as I walked through the press box. I looked around and saw my favorite *Los Angeles Times* writer working on his typewriter. I was escorted to a table in the back, where dinner was waiting for us. I walked past the empty chair where Vin had faithfully and colorfully called Dodgers games for sixty years. He rose from the table, extended his right hand, and said, "Hello, John."

Over dinner, I asked him questions about his mentors, religious convictions (a devout Catholic who reads his Bible every single day), the Hall of Fame, and Jackie Robinson and issues of race. He made it a point to predict that Asian players would break into the Major Leagues and become sensational stars in America. Today the audiocassette recording of my dinner interview with Vin Scully is one of my prized possessions (though I no longer have the ability to play it).

And since I know you're wondering, yes, I received an A on the term paper.

That interview makes me consider my relationship with God. While we've never met God face-to-face, we do know his character. Our lives are full of rejection letters from publicists, but we must be careful never to attribute rejection and the resulting despair to God. The 72 live in the reality that when we boldly approach him, he is patient, kind, offering a listening ear, and asking us, "What can I do for you?" My heart is encouraged by these words of Darrell Johnson: "We often say, or hear said, 'Prayer works.' That is only so because the one to whom we pray works."[2]

As you reflect on your life of prayer, do you believe God is too busy for us? Do you believe he's distant and unapproachable? Do you believe that the great burdens that overwhelm your heart and mind are foreign to him?

Jesus taught the 72 that not only is prayer real, but the One who answers prayer is really, really good. He wants to have dinner with his children. He wants us to join him in his work. So God first taught the 72 how to pray.

HABITS OF THE 72: EARNEST PRAYER

As you consider a lifestyle of earnestly praying to the Lord of the harvest, I encourage you to consider seven prayer tips. I believe these will increase and enhance your intimacy with God and your ministry of evangelism:

1. *Pray daily.* Earnest prayer includes a consistent prayer life. Make a commitment to pray every day for evangelism. We spend time with those we love. And Jesus loves spending time with us.

2. *Have a regular location.* When you pray, go to the same place every day. Jesus prayed regularly at a lonely place. Find and create a place that's comfortable, that's free of distractions, and that enhances your intimacy with God.

3. *Listen.* When you pray, listen for the voice of God. The living God is not like the false gods Bel and Nebo (Isaiah 46:1). He is alive, dynamic, and loves to speak to his children. Begin times of prayer by asking God questions and listening for his voice.

4. *Ask for friends.* If you have trouble making new friends, ask the Lord of the harvest to bring you new friends. God is at work in the lives of so many unbelievers. He is faithful to bring people to his evangelists.

5. *Keep records.* Write down your prayers. The more specific the better. Include person, date, location, any Scripture associated with your prayer, and any communication from the Holy Spirit. Review the lists to see if God has yet answered them.

6. *Ask for power.* The New Testament power gifts are given by God to authenticate the message of the gospel. Pray for those power gifts (Ephesians 4:8-12). One display of God's power in the life of a non-Christian can bring him or her to faith immediately. Be willing to pray with and for your non-Christian friends for healing, provision, and demonic issues. They are likely far more open to prayer than you might think.

7. *Rejoice.* After every evangelistic conversation or new commitment, I say to my soul, "Rejoice that your name is written

in heaven." If the evangelistic conversation goes well, this keeps me from pride and focusing on ministry results. If the conversation goes poorly, this keeps me from shame and the residual effects of rejection.

LUKE AND TWO MODELS OF PRAYER

In the book of Luke are many models of prayer. The subject alone warrants careful study and an entirely new book. I think of Mary choosing the better portion and sitting at the feet of the Lord. Hers was a prayer of personal devotion. The tax collector beating his breast in an act of contrition and loathing of his sinful state is a prayer of self-examination and confession. The Gospel of Luke concludes with the disciples on the Emmaus Road jubilant and full of worship as they discovered for themselves that Jesus of Nazareth was truly God become flesh and that all he said and promised was true. This is a prayer of adoration. Time constrains our ability to dive into each methodology of prayer, but I'd like to highlight two models of prayer in Luke that help us and our friends experience the kingdom.

PRAYERS OF INTERCESSION

And there was a prophetess, Anna, the daughter of Phanuel, of the tribe of Asher. She was advanced in years, having lived with her husband seven years from when she was a virgin, and then as a widow until she was eighty-four. She did not depart from the temple, worshiping with fasting and prayer night and day. (Luke 2:36-37)

Anna, the prophetess, modeled intercessory prayer. Daily she brought others and their needs before God. This woman of faith spent all of her life in the temple, worshiping God through fasting and prayers. As someone who knew the goodness of God, she couldn't help but be in his presence. It's remarkable that Luke would bestow upon someone with so little earthly honor the immortalization of her life and ministry through Scripture. I think of all the people, churches, denominations, and mission agencies that Anna has encouraged for the last two thousand years. Her prayers not only ushered in the arrival of the living God in human form, but they offered a model that has helped build the kingdom long after she departed the temple.

Earnest prayers of intercession change history. Again, it is a great mystery how the living God stirs us to pray and moves through those prayers to fulfill his great plans. As I consider FOL, my heart is forever grateful to Mrs. Elaine Powers. She's a fifth-grade teacher at Webster Elementary, the school right behind our house. The school has many problems, and it often ranks among the lowest-performing schools in the district in the academic categories. Many of the students and families try their best but struggle with learning a new language, working multiple jobs, trying to get their lives on track, and staying out of trouble. But Mrs. Powers and her fellow Dual Immersion teachers are bright and shining stars in West Long Beach.

Mrs. Powers, an African American woman, is fluent in Spanish and has taught the Spanish-English fifth-grade class for twenty years. My niece and nephew grew tremendously in her class. And her teaching ministry blessed our daughter Joy. Mrs. Powers has seen everything an inner-city school can throw at her, and she's stronger for the challenge. She loves the children with grace and truth, and she lives out her faith boldly.

In the late 1990s and early 2000s, West Long Beach and Webster Elementary were in a particularly dark place. Violence was the norm at Springdale, children were underperforming, gang recruiting and teen pregnancies were at peak numbers, and according to Mrs. Powers, there was a cloud of darkness over the neighborhood. So she called together her fellow Christian teachers and said that they must pray. They committed to the Lord and to one another and met regularly to pray for West Long Beach.

At a recent church anniversary celebration, God encouraged us by having Mrs. Powers and her wonderful family attend our service. She took the microphone, looked at our auditorium, looked at the sixty youth at the service—many of whom she had taught, was teaching then, or would teach—and began to speak. Her voice cracked a bit as her normally polished delivery was affected by a wave of emotion. She finally said, "FOL, we have been praying for you to be here for many, many years. I can't believe that God created a church just down the street from Webster Elementary. Praise Jesus!"

I firmly believe that our call to plant FOL is a direct connection to prayers of intercession. Mrs. Power prayed earnestly for kingdom workers to come to West Long Beach. The Lord of the harvest answered her prayers and sent us to plant FOL.

PRAYING FOR KINGDOM WORKERS

I am a Christian today because a woman prayed Luke 10 prayers for me. During my first year at UCLA, God sovereignly chose Keren Ji to be my dormitory neighbor. Keren's prayers changed my life and eternal destiny.

As I mentioned, I lived a wild life before committing to Christ. During my first ten-week quarter in the dorms, I was written up five times for various alcohol-related and dorm vandalism violations. My friends and I would often return from the bars at two in the morning and play full-contact basketball in my dorm room. My roommate hated when we did that, and I'm sure Keren, who slept on the other side of our paper-thin walls, didn't appreciate it either.

During week two that first quarter, Keren kindly reminded me that she had classes at eight in the morning, but I didn't care.

As I became a growing problem in her life, Keren, a Christian who had developed her faith in a strong Korean church, turned to God and prayer. The Holy Spirit spoke to her and gave her kingdom eyes to see me with. She saw me as someone who was hopelessly lost, needing God, and needing prayer. In week four of our fall quarter, she committed to praying for God to send me an evangelist. She prayed for me every single day.

Shortly after she began praying, Dave Palmer, an InterVarsity student leader, befriended me and invited me into his Bible study. Five months later, I became a follower of Jesus. I attribute much of my conversion to Keren and her faithful prayers. She saw me as someone who was "ripe for harvest," and God sent a kingdom worker to me.

I converted in May, and the academic year ended in June. As we moved out of the dorm, we said we would stay in touch. But at such a large school, and before the days of social media, I didn't see Keren for the next three years at UCLA. I bet she wondered more than once if I had continued on the rigorous path of discipleship.

Four years later, I saw Keren at Urbana 96, InterVarsity Christian Fellowship's missions conference in Urbana, Illinois. The evening plenary session had just released, and twenty thousand students and I moved out into the cold, snowy night to the buses. As I stood in line, I heard someone say, "John?" It was Keren. She was there leading her church's college group into world missions. And she was shocked to see me. The last time we'd seen each other, I was a thirty-day-old Christian. I told her I was now a campus minister with InterVarsity. Knowing where I had come from and what I had been through, she was so happy she began to cry. I hugged her and thanked her for praying to the Lord of the harvest for me.

KINGDOM WORKERS AND UPS

When the 72 first gathered for their evangelism training, I doubt prayer was their first action plan. Yet this was their spiritual preparation for the mission. People in Hong Kong, people in West Long Beach, and lost college students vandalizing dorms all need kingdom workers to deliver the gospel. A generic message is not enough. God sends people to people to deliver the gospel. Just as Amazon works because UPS faithfully and consistently delivers packages, we must rely on the Lord of the harvest, asking him for more workers.

Our prayers will work because the One we pray to is always working.

NEXT STEP: Please visit folantioch.org/resources to access training videos on evangelism.

FEATURED VIDEO: *How to Keep a Dynamic Prayer Journal*

6

FRIENDS:

SECULAR TO SACRED

The first Bible people will read is your life.

REBECCA PIPPERT

ME AND JULIO DOWN BY THE BALL YARD

I met "Julio" at one of my son Luke's Little League games. I was one of the coaches and was behind home plate, filming the action. Julio was on the other side of the fence. He was wearing the jersey of one of my favorite wide receivers, so between innings I struck up a conversation about fantasy football. He told me he was in ten leagues, yet his wife "didn't trip," because he had won five and given her the money. I'm in only one league, and it's a high-commitment endeavor. I asked him which players were sleepers, which outperformed their draft pick, and which under-performed or busted. We had a similar bust player, so we shared about how smart he was supposed to make us look. It was nice sharing our failures and frustrations.

I know this conversation may mean very little to many readers, but I include it as an example of meeting people where they are. Julio was a fantasy sports fanatic. Luckily, I knew something about that, and our conversation led to a great deal of connection and trust. If Julio were into cars (which I know nothing about), I would have asked him questions, found a connection point, and continued from there.

I enjoy meeting new people, but because I know I'm part of the 72, I also have a few goals in mind. As I engage in conversation, I attempt to discern how the Spirit of God may be at work drawing the person to Christ. Answering this question is part feeling and part fact. I never know until I'm in the middle of the conversation which way it will go, but I'm always encouraged when people ask questions.

I also seek the Holy Spirit's leading. In the encounter with Julio, the conversation progressed rapidly. I let him know I was a pastor, and he didn't respond or create extra barriers for our interaction. I told him a few things about my life and my fantasy football interest in good wide receivers and pass-catching running backs, which seemed to interest him. Next I felt the Holy Spirit urge me, so I invited him over for dinner. One of my personal ministry insights is that people more readily accept an invitation to your home for Bible study if they've been there before for purely social reasons.

So, yes, I invited Julio and his very large family for dinner. We hung out, we ate some great food from 5000 Pies (the social enterprise restaurant my wife started for our church), the kids ran around, and we all had a blast. A few days later, Julio emailed me, saying, "Pastor John, being in your home and eating with your family was awesome. You are a good man for opening up your home."

There is great power in food, hospitality, and building spiritual friendships.

CHAPTER THEME: The 72 were trained for spiritual friendships.

CORE TEXT: Luke 10:4-8

Carry no moneybag, no knapsack, no sandals, and greet no one on the road. Whatever house you enter, first say, "Peace be to this house!" And if a son of peace is there, your peace will rest upon him. But if not, it will return to you. And remain in the same house, eating and drinking what they provide, for the laborer deserves his wages. Do not go from house to house. Whenever you enter a town and they receive you, eat what is set before you.

Jesus placed the 72 into positions where they were dependent on new relationships. They were told to leave their wallets, their purses, and their credit cards at home. They were to blow right past other people ("greet no one on the road," v. 4) who might slow them down. Because the 72 had very little in the way of practical comforts, they depended on new people for survival. In *The IVP Bible Background Commentary*, Craig Keener wrote, "It was offensive to withhold greetings, and pious people tried to be the first to greet an approaching person."[1] Yet Jesus taught them to break the rule of cultural hospitality. This underscores the urgency and primacy of the call to make new friends for the sake of evangelism.

I realize that many of us have a hard time making friends and that it's harder for some of us to build friendships with non-Christians. I once attended an evangelism conference where the speaker led the audience in an exercise to determine how many non-Christian friends we had called on our phones recently. With great conviction and fire, the speaker admonished the crowd that if we really love Jesus, we have non-Christians up and down our call history. There was an audible gasp, as I'm sure many felt convicted. In retrospect, however, I don't think it's that simple. Evangelists tend to be good with people and have strong communication skills, so they are quickly recruited to leadership roles within ministries and become recognized leaders.

In the kingdom of God, the reward for excellent work is not retirement. The reward for fruitful work is more fruitful work

(Luke 19:17). My friend Dave Olson and his coauthor, Craig Groe-schel, wrote in *The American Church in Crisis*, "The problem with fruitful ministry is there is much fruit to take care of."[2] While it's good and right to challenge people to have more space in their lives for the lost, it's a bit more complicated when each individual is a faithful leader in a Christian ministry. In creating more space in our lives for non-Christians, we must be creative and even ruthless with the ways we allocate our time.

I love that Jesus cleared the calendar, the responsibilities, and the normal ministry tasks of the 72. When he called, they canceled everything to participate in the training day, the field mission, and the ministry tour debrief. The 72 received a new vision, training, and—of equal importance—a free calendar to engage fully in that vision. For many of us, the idea of adding a new network of friends seems emotionally overwhelming. There's simply no room on the calendar. If we are to live as one of the 72, we need more space, more time, and more energy to meet new people. The evangelist who keeps adding to the ministry vision and workload, never pruning back for more fruitful ministry, can never "travel light, taking only what they need on their mission journey," Keener wrote.[3] May you draw great strength from the precedent of Jesus clearing the calendars of his anonymous evangelists.

PROCESS CONVERSION TIMELINE

After Jesus taught the 72 to pray earnestly for more kingdom workers, he gave them their first ministry task: use the mission tool of food to get an accurate read on how far their friend was away from the kingdom of God. To put it another way, Jesus taught them how to eat with non-Christians while being detectives investi-gating the spiritual foundations of their new friends.

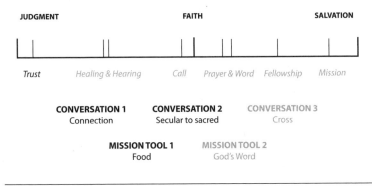

Figure 6.1. Conversion process timeline

WHATEVER HOUSE YOU ENTER

Jesus taught his seventy-two missionaries to visit people in their homes. This is very significant for us too. We aren't called to set up a religious stand on the corner and hit them over their heads with information. The home is where evangelism finds its footing. To host someone or meet someone at home is to get to know that person on a much deeper level. When we're inside another person's home, it's a practical reminder that no other person in the history of the world is exactly like that person. There has never been another human that liked the exact same things or had the exact same experiences. When we're in the homes of our friends, we find ourselves sharing in the families, the hobbies, and the benchmark moments of each person.

For centuries, the Christian tradition of hospitality has been how the church has cared for the most vulnerable people in society. Through the consistent and ever-deepening commitment of hospitality, we understand the physical, emotional, and spiritual needs of the people we're reaching. In a home, where we share and enjoy food, bonds develop. Jan Martinez said this about her experiences of outreach through a social enterprise restaurant in San Francisco:

"Hospitality was the key means by which the church responded to the physical needs of strangers for food, shelter and protection. Hospitality recognized the worth and common humanity of every person."[4]

On a practical level, what does this look like? In communities, developing trust takes time. To invite myself to a neighbor's home would be presumptuous on many levels. Maybe he isn't open to having guests in his home, or she feels that her apartment isn't nice enough for company. Some homes are overcrowded, and others have activity going on that the inhabitants don't want a pastor to know about.

Because I would never invite myself over to someone's home, I never participate in door-to-door evangelism. When people are home, especially on a weekend, they aren't looking for someone to bother them, because they're making pancakes with the kids, for example. Of course, if we're invited, we certainly accept the invitation.

Our church makes us available to the Holy Spirit on evangelism days. We go to public places like our local park or go for long, prayerful walks and see who God brings to us. Invariably the Lord of the harvest does lead us to someone he is at work in. Occasionally we are even invited into that person's home, and relationship grows from there.

EAT WHAT IS BEFORE YOU

Hospitality goes hand in hand with food, so it's no coincidence that Jesus focused on food. In Luke's Gospel, the references to the ministry of hospitality and the table where bread is broken are so prevalent, they seem to be another character. Many of Jesus' greatest moments of outreach and teaching happened at table during a meal.

- *Luke 5:29.* "And Levi made him a great feast in his house, and there was a large company of tax collectors and others reclining at table with them."

- *Luke 7:36-37.* "One of the Pharisees asked him to eat with him, and he went into the Pharisee's house and reclined at table. And behold, a woman of the city, who was a sinner, when she learned that he was reclining at table in the Pharisee's house, brought an alabaster flask of ointment."

- *Luke 13:29.* "And people will come from east and west, and from north and south, and recline at table in the kingdom of God."

- *Luke 14:10.* "But when you are invited, go and sit in the lowest place, so that when your host comes he may say to you, 'Friend, move up higher.' Then you will be honored in the presence of all who sit at table with you."

- *Luke 14:15.* "When one of those who reclined at table with him heard these things, he said to him, 'Blessed is everyone who will eat bread in the kingdom of God!'"

- *Luke 22:27.* "For who is the greater, one who reclines at table or one who serves? Is it not the one who reclines at table? But I am among you as the one who serves."

- *Luke 24:30.* "When he was at table with them, he took the bread and blessed and broke it and gave it to them."

You can change someone's eternal destiny by eating together. No matter what age, socioeconomic status, political alignment, or theological background, every person has to eat. And there's a great power in breaking bread with one another. At the table, every person's worth, dignity, and value are affirmed. In many Asian cultures, the family dinner table is a circle, emphasizing their shared life together and the equal value of all people, no matter the person's status, gender, or age. All our special contributions are shared with the community at the table. Even though the poor have limited resources and status, fellowship is experienced abundantly, and loving friendships are established.

The table is the perfect place for the 72 to build trust and to initiate conversations. Whenever I sit down for a meal with someone I don't know well, I immediately think of the television show *Law & Order*. This is the longest-running series in the history of television, and it has unapologetically had the same structure for over twenty-five years. There's no need to apologize when a formula works! During the first eight minutes, a crime is discovered, and detectives ask witnesses what they saw. Becky and I always joke that the witnesses are always either disrespectful or aloof when being questioned. The detectives ask all their questions, listen carefully, look intently, and write everything down in their notebooks.

Every time a scene changes, the show drops its memorable sound effect, called "The Clang" by the composer. If you've ever watched one episode of *Law & Order*, you know what I mean. "Dun dun."

Of course, being a spiritual detective isn't confined to the dinner table, but it's much easier logistically than talking on a subway, at the water cooler at work, or while chasing kids in the park. And Jesus instructed the 72 to use a spiritual diagnostic tool to see if those they met were far from the kingdom of God: move on to the next relationship if "the peace does not return to you." I interpret that Jewish idiom in our own culture today to mean that we are to move on if the Spirit of God is not at work—yet.

CONVERSION CONVERSATION 1: INITIAL INVESTIGATION

Herein lies the great temptation of the first stage of connection. All of us like to be liked, and we love to be loved. None of us wants to be rejected, persecuted, or thrown into the forest with a hungry grizzly bear. So, in the name of building trust and bonding over food, we can lose our focus and courage, and our relationship becomes like any other. We begin with a vision for relational evangelism, but too often we stop at "relational." It's fun and exciting to bond with new friends, eat at cool places, and drop Yelp reviews together. But that isn't the mission. We must investigate to see how God is at work in their lives.

This may not be a popular teaching today, but relationships are both an end and a means. What ministry assignment doesn't include people? As we consider evangelism, we must become more skilled, more aware, and more fruitful in building relationships. But these relationships aren't to be an end in and of themselves. God doesn't want you to be friends with non-Christians so that a mere friendship happens. Relationships are the God-ordained vehicle for transferring faith. God chooses to win to discipleship through relationships.

Relationships are never meant to cure our loneliness or the loneliness of others, though they most certainly help. We abide in Christ, and he's the one who meets all our needs. We must always keep the call to evangelism in front of us. There's a dire need in local churches for evangelism. Without successful evangelism, we will never fulfill the final charge of Jesus that disciples "go and make disciples." Instead, the great command of Jesus is watered down into trying to take care of people who are already Christian. Or we deconstruct the call to be one of the 72 in the lives of others, and we settle for human community yet call it the ministry of evangelism.

HABITS OF THE 72: SPIRITUAL DETECTIVES

To make certain we're doing the hard work of evangelism, here are seven habits for spiritual detectives. Living these habits has helped me stay centered in the vision of the 72.

1. *Leave the office.* If you're a church leader, you can't meet unbelievers behind the desk in your office. If you're in another

type of work, you can't either. Paul went to the river and met Lydia (Acts 16:13-14). The riverbank served as a community gathering spot where he could instigate for faith. Be available in community gathering spots.

2. *Put it on the calendar.* If you don't put relational evangelism on the calendar, it will be hard to make yourself available to meet new people. Be disciplined to schedule it, and consider it an appointment with the Holy Spirit.

3. *Go in twos.* Jesus sent the 72 out in pairs. When you go in twos, you have built-in accountability, encouragement, and learning. Give each other feedback as you meet new people. Evangelism is better when we're together.

4. *Have confidence.* When he was on trial, the apostle Paul told King Felix and the entire Roman court, "I wish you were all like me" (see Acts 26:29). If he walked into a Starbucks, he would be overflowing with confidence (and concern) toward lost sinners. He would not shrink back. We must live our lives like we've won the lottery, because in the next dimension, we have.

5. *Assume people are open.* God has been at work in the lives of our friends since long before we met them. Assume he's at work as you meet new people. Look for clues to whom you should be talking to.

6. *Small talk.* Learn to speak on a new-acquaintance level. Look for connection points, and ask questions based on current events, entertainment, sports, or common interests you might observe. If you aren't comfortable with this, learn from your friends in the service industries (waiters, baristas). I learned the art of small talk by working at a tennis center.

7. *Ask detective questions.* After gaining trust, I ask one simple question. Do not try to be clever; be clear. I usually ask something

like this: "I have really enjoyed our friendship, but I know so little about your spiritual background. Have you had any spiritual signs or any church background?" And then I just listen (as I hear the *Law & Order* soundbite in my head). I'm often amazed at how God has already been at work in the person. I often follow up with the question "Do you have any questions about God, Jesus, or the Bible?" And I keep listening.

CONVERSION CONVERSATION 2: SECULAR TO SACRED

After eating with and investigating the spiritual life of your non-Christian friend, you should have a thirty-thousand-foot overview of her spiritual background. At this stage, you'll hopefully begin to feel the need to deepen the relationship from the secular to the sacred. This is a very good development. While it might cause some anxiety and even fear, it's a sign God is at work in your friend. It's time for the second conversion conversation to help her experience the Word of God for herself.

For a season, I tried to ask clever questions and use complex metaphors. The results were terrible. The words got all jumbled up. I felt self-conscious. Friends were often confused, so I ditched the clever to focus on the clear.

I begin the conversation by requesting a more formal, sit-down conversation. This grabs my friends' attention with a healthy mix of fear and curiosity. They wonder if they did something wrong or if there's something really big going down. When we sit down for the conversation, I usually begin with an affirmation of God's work in our friendship, such as, "It has been such a joy getting to know you better. I thank God for bringing us together."

I then say that there's something on my heart, but I'm afraid I might be judged for it. This is honest, and it helps them see me as a real and vulnerable human being. I make it a point to ask for permission to share what's on my heart, and I say, "I want to ask you an important spiritual question, but I don't want to put any strain on our relationship. And I certainly don't want you to think I'm being aggressive or pushy."

Nine times out of every ten, the person is relieved that I'm talking about our spiritual lives. They're in the position of power and aren't on their heels in fear of me becoming an overly zealous evangelist. Almost every time, they say they would love to hear my question.

So, again, I choose clear over clever when I ask, "Would you be interested in joining me in a personal study of the Scripture? You will grow in faith, learn a lot, and I really think you would like Jesus." I'm prepared for them to say yes. We get a date on the calendar to meet together and study the Word. I give them a page with the verse from the Bible study that we will study. I give them minimal direction for spiritual homework, and I model for them that it's okay to write on the page and list their questions. After this conversation, the friendship has officially moved from the secular to the sacred.

To close the chapter, I offer two examples of secular friendships progressing to an invitation to explore the sacred and both of those processes being terminated.

JULIO

I opened the chapter with the story of Julio coming over for dinner. He and his wife took a big step after our second conversion conversation: joining our Bible study. I thought things were going well, but after three studies, giant walls went up. He began calling me with intense questions about church, his vocation, and leadership issues. An issue came up in his relationship with someone else in our study, and he exploded, threatening my friend physical harm. When I tried to sit down with him, he blew up on me, questioning my motives, slandering my character, and calling me terrible names. Long gone was the affirmation of "you are a good man."

There's no happy ending to the story at this point. I've seen him twice at the baseball park this season. He doesn't talk to me. Jesus tells us that we are like a sheep among wolves, so we don't put our hope in ministry results. I rejoice that my name is written in heaven.

THE CHILLY EXAMINATION ROOM

I met Dr. Young a few years ago when I experienced knee problems after playing tennis. I'm learning the hard way that getting old has many kingdom-of-God benefits, but few physical ones. My tennis mileage caught up to me, requiring Dr. Young to perform a surgical repair of my slightly torn meniscus. We had a nice connection but developing a spiritual friendship never happened.

Recently I suffered the single biggest injury of my life: I ruptured my Achilles tendon while playing tennis. It's excruciatingly painful, requires corrective surgery, and promises an intense four months of rehabilitation. Dr. Young and I saw each other three times in one month. On the second visit, I threw out connection points to gauge gospel interest. On my last visit, with Easter coming up, I took a more proactive approach. I told him I was preaching an Easter sermon that was right up his alley. Its theme was Jesus describing himself to the scribes and the Pharisees as the good physician for sick sinners. I asked him if he'd ever heard that Jesus called himself the spiritual physician. The doctor looked me in the eye for three seconds and said nothing. The examination room got a bit colder.

I was already in the deep end, so I just went for it. I held out our church flyer and said, "I plan to speak about my rehabilitation process and how I'm trying to follow your prescription. I would love for you to come and hear me teach the Bible." My arm stayed extended.

He looked at the flyer and made no attempt to grab it. He then reported with no emotion, "My family is going to Mammoth this weekend. My kids love to ski." And that's how it ended. The examination was over. His final words to me were, "Be sure to book your followup appointment on the way out."

On the drive home, I prayed to God about this conversation with Dr. Young. I asked him to send kingdom workers to Dr. Young, even on the chairlifts of Mammoth as he skied. I also told God I didn't appreciate being blown off by my orthopedic surgeon. I then closed my prayer time thanking God that I wasn't the one being rejected; Dr. Young had apparently rejected God. I thank God that my name is written in heaven.

ADULT ESL OUTREACH CLASS

Caroline Sato is one of the founding members of FOL. She has learned Spanish as a second language in order to reach out and make disciples among our Spanish-speaking neighbors. Drawing upon her education background, she began a new ministry teaching English. Her first class attracted thirty adults. The classes run Monday through Thursday, and Friday is an optional Bible study so people can study the Word for themselves. Here is her testimony of moving her friends from secular to the sacred:

> My story is the story of how God took twenty-five years of seemingly unrelated experiences and brought them together in one ministry. I had, in those twenty-five years, learned to teach inductive Bible studies, although I didn't like it much. I had learned to cook and bake for crowds of people. I had been an adult educator for fifteen years and had become fluent in Spanish almost by accident. I had never, ever intended to become a minister of the Word in Spanish to women in West Long Beach.

But here I am, meeting weekly with a group of ten students from my ESL class. What I didn't know when I started four years ago is that all my life has been tending toward this ministry. I hadn't enjoyed teaching the Bible in English in college, but for some reason, in Spanish, I love it. And so do the students! Far from having to draw them out, I have had to figure out how to end the studies in under three hours. Praying out loud in Spanish terrified me at first, but our weekly prayers for each other are a consistent source of God's grace poured out to our group. And each week I bake! Food is an important part of our life together.

Some lovely life transformations have sprung from the study. Josefina, who was almost literally dragged in off the street to her first study by another member, has seen her whole family transformed. This generous woman was in the process of adopting her grandson Ángel because her estranged daughter could not care for him. But she was overwhelmed by the prospect of raising him. We began to pray, and she brought him to church. He loved it, to her surprise. They came every week, and soon her husband, Rubén, came with her. Then Rubén started taking English classes with me, and he came to the Bible study as well. Not long after that, Josefina's daughter found herself pregnant again; she began rehab and came to church as well. She came to Jesus at FOL and was baptized last year; the baby is well and happy; and the whole family has reconciled to God and each other. Ángel is currently the second baseman on John's Farm Ball Little League team.

Some students had been around God their whole lives, but as they began to read the Word for themselves, they latched onto Jesus like never before. My former student Ana is in this category. Much like me, she grew up as a Catholic with a decent theology but without a solid foundation in the Word. She grew up seeing God primarily as a rule-giver. Reading the Gospels closely has brought depth to her faith as she knows more of God's character. She also has grown in relating personally to Jesus as her close friend, not a far-off concept. What a delight it is to simply give to her the gift of inductive study that was given to me in my teens!

Lastly, one student who had deep faith but an incomplete picture of God is Herlinda. When I met her, she was a somewhat fearful person, anxious about her sons, about money, about accidents and illness. She also had deep bitterness toward some members of her family. Over two years or so, she wrestled hard with the Word—so hard, in fact, that I thought she disagreed with much of what Jesus said. But then one day she announced that she had forgiven her sister-in-law. Another day she told us she no longer feared death. "Death? Were you sick?" people asked. "No, but I used to be afraid my sons would get hurt or I would die young. Now I'm not. I say Psalm 91 to myself and I believe it. When I say good-bye to them, I don't worry if they'll come back home. I feel peaceful." Today Herlinda brings her family to FOL every Sunday, and she works as one of the primary cooks for 5000 Pies. The Lord's transformation in her life is truly incredible.

Some of our friends are open to moving their relationship from the secular to the sacred. Others are not. Jesus trained the 72 to bring Josefina, Ana, and Herlinda to faith. And he trained the 72 to be rejected by Julio, Dr. Young, and all the others who reject the One who sends us. Without Conversion Conversation 2 and monitoring how they respond to an invitation and/or the Word, we would never know if they wish to put their faith in Jesus.

NEXT STEP: Please visit folantioch.org/resources for the "Antioch Academy Class: 72."

FEATURED VIDEO: *Answering Seven Hard Questions Nonbelievers Are Asking*

FEATURED RESOURCE: "Secular to Sacred Without Freaking Out Your Friends"

EXPERIENCE:
HEALING AND HEARING

Note that the emblem was not only fire, but a tongue
of fire, for God meant to have a speaking church.

CHARLES SPURGEON

MY FIRST EVANGELISTIC BIBLE STUDY

look back with great fondness as I consider my own development
as an evangelist and teacher. Twenty-five years ago, I committed
to teaching the Word of God to my friends. We all start at the
same place, so you can also make this commitment to God. My
first years of discipleship were far more about what God was doing
in me than through me, as it is for all of us. In the experience of
putting my name, reputation, and faith on the line, I became more
loyal and more in love with Jesus. I rejoice that my name is written
in heaven.

I didn't grow up in a Christian home. But after I became a
Christian, I returned home from college to my very irreligious band
of partiers. I was excited to share about my conversion and about
all I was learning about Jesus. Some unbelieving friends were intrigued that something spiritual was clearly happening to me. My

friend Norman would come around and ask me to say a prayer for him, "to the big guy upstairs."

My first attempt at evangelism was to start a Bible study for my friends. I had been a Christian for all of six weeks. I knew very little, but with a lot of grit and faith, I made catchy fliers based on hip-hop music, promised great food, and invited all my friends. I prayed harder than I had ever prayed, asking God to bring my friends to Bible study.

Our first study was·on a Saturday morning at my friend Jeff's house. His parents were in Palm Springs for the weekend. The night before, he had hosted a five-keg party for four hundred people. The party had gotten out of hand and was broken up by the police. They even sent in the helicopter, which was big news in Hacienda Heights.

Three of my friends were hauled off to jail that night, so I crossed them off my Bible study RSVP list. Most of my friends spent the night at Jeff's, and some rolled out of bed just in time to make the noon study. A couple of them hadn't slept all night due to a cocaine binge and were both wired and tired. Tony Montana from *Scarface* would have felt right at home when I distributed the Bible text.

Today I'm amazed that twenty very unchurched people came to my first Bible study. The study itself was terrible. Norman, who loved geometry, thought Jesus taught in parabolas, not parables. When I asked my friends to consider what soil type they were from the Mark 4 parable, Susan openly challenged me. "John, I don't care what soil type I am. Stop judging me!" Totally baffled, I immediately ended the study with an awkward prayer. But at least the food was great. My mom had prepared it for all of us.

I now realize that these first efforts at evangelism were critical moments in my growth as an evangelist. I had stumbled onto a format of how to make new disciples. At FOL, we like to ask,

"Where is the best place for a non-Christian to convert?" Sometimes people answer with real physical locations, like the beach or the Christian camp in the mountains. Those who are more progressive might say Starbucks. Of course, this is a trick question. The best place for a non-Christian to convert is in a small-group Bible study. In a study, they have trusted friends and built-in pastoral leadership to help them grow and learn from the Word.

Twenty-five years ago, I learned about evangelistic Bible studies, a methodology that's essential to making and deepening new disciples today. My instincts taught me that our friends must hear the gospel for themselves. I just wasn't very good at teaching Bible studies yet. Twenty-five years later, I'm still learning. Jesus taught—and continually teaches—the 72 to heal the city and teach the Word.

CHAPTER THEME: Jesus trains the 72 for evangelism in word and deed.

CORE TEXT: Exegesis of Luke 10:9

> *Heal the sick in it and say to them, "The kingdom of God has come near to you."*

The 72 are sent to heal the sick and proclaim the kingdom of God. I love that Jesus trains his evangelists to meet all the needs of those they minister to. Yes, there are many who are sick in the city. Physical illness, mental illness, addiction, broken relationships, and cycles of urban poverty are but a few of the "healing issues" urban evangelists face today. We're called to get into the lives of those we break bread with and to be agents of healing as we connect them to Jesus and the vast natural and supernatural resources he generously offers to sinners and saints alike.

And we are called to be the speaking church. Meeting physical, emotional, and socioeconomic needs is never enough. Those we minister to need to be people of faith. Our friends will not be judged on if they ate better, lost weight, controlled their blood pressure, helped their kids get to college, or became great soccer coaches. They will be judged—like every human being who ever lived on planet Earth—based on how they responded to Jesus of Nazareth, the firstborn of the new humanity, who offers intimacy and life in God.

The tension between doing good and telling the truth is not new. The church has always had to manage the relationship of love and word, demonstration and declaration. In the Lausanne Covenant, a 1974 agreement focusing on worldwide evangelization, theologian John Stott spoke powerfully on the need for balance. Paul Borthwick deftly handles this matter in his book *Great Commission, Great Compassion*, drawing lessons and parallels from Matthew 28 and 25.

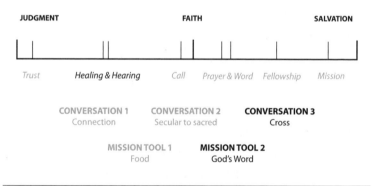

Figure 7.1. Conversion process timeline

BALANCE AND HEALING THE SICK

From my perspective as a church planter, pastor, and network leader, a balance of deed and word is our goal. With this pithy two-step command in Luke 10:9, Jesus instructed his disciples that both love and word are needed for effective mission. If the 72 only heal the sick in the city, they meet only short-term needs. But a good life means nothing when the last breath is taken and faith is the ultimate need. But if the 72 neglect any of the needs and only focus on proclaiming the message, they come off as tone-deaf zealots, and the teaching has little resonance or meaning to those still stuck in their pain. In FOL, we have a mantra that highlights the need for both word and deed: "Good deeds lead to good will; and good will leads to good news." When the 72 are sent out, they operate with a balanced vision of meeting practical needs and teaching eternal truth.

As I observe the Christian ministry landscape today, I believe the default of most Christians is to "do good." The pendulum is swinging hard toward the do-good side, and I fear we equate this with fruitful ministry. I recently received a call from a church planter who was seeking wisdom to lead his affluent congregation into a social enterprise. We discussed Luke 10:9 as the balanced vision of the Lord for these outreach matters. And I asked many questions to better understand his vision.

It basically came down to the pastor hoping to create a church-owned grocery store to provide an alternative for the suburban community he was reaching out to. "Doing good" for this congregation meant trying to undercut the outrageous price of organic corn. After a half-hour of careful listening on the phone, I asked if I could speak a word of balance. I tried to share compassionately my belief that his community didn't need a more Christian version of Trader Joe's. Let's give unto Caesar what is Caesar's, even if the romaine lettuce prices are ridiculous, but we must be certain to give unto God what is God's.

With social enterprises being so popular at the moment, it's easy to confuse a Christian-based business or social service with true Christian ministry. I fear that many today are giving their lives to meeting needs in the name of "healing the city," but after the enormous costs, years of service, and emotional grind of difficult ministry, there will be no new disciples.

The second factor in Jesus' balanced approach is that, like all of his commands, obedience drives out unbelief in our hearts and lives. If Jesus hadn't instructed his 72 to tell the story of the gospel, I believe the idol of fear would win the day in the hearts of many Christians. We live in a world that punishes people personally, vocationally, and on social media for saying what might be construed as politically incorrect. No one has ever spoken like Jesus, and he himself was persecuted unto death for speaking truth.

A quotation attributed to St. Francis of Assisi says: "Preach the gospel at all times. If necessary, use words." When I hear that, I wonder if Francis's larger ministry context emphasized speaking the word over service and acts of love. If that's the case, it's an entirely appropriate exhortation to strengthen a weak area of ministry. In our era, I believe many Christians have given themselves over to fear. We must heed the most repeated exhortation in the New Testament, "Do not be afraid," and open our mouths to proclaim the kingdom. We must choose obedience.

Yes, we are called to heal the sick as well as feed and clothe the poor in our city. On the communal and nonprofit ministry level, I applaud the amazing efforts of so many creative, strong, and wonderful Christian ministries. God is doing a great work to open doors for kingdom workers to proclaim the gospel. And the good deeds are certainly leading to good will.

I also believe we need to be challenged to live more fully into the power of the Holy Spirit to heal. Upon their return, the 72 rejoiced beyond measure that the demons were subject to them because of Jesus' name (Luke 10:17).

JUNIOR

The morning of December 7, 2014, started like every school morning for our family. The children ate breakfast, got their clothes ready, brushed and combed their hair and teeth, and together as a family we walked to Webster Elementary School. I walked Kara down the hallway to her transitional kindergarten class, kissed her good-bye, and watched her rush into her classroom with her oversize backpack. Suddenly, I heard Kara's teacher, Mrs. Lipiz, call out, "Pastor Teter! Pastor Teter!" (She loves God and ministers to the students and families of Webster. She has been to our church and loves to partner with us to help people experience God.)

She continued to call out my name while standing next to a parent I had never met, named Junior Alfonso. She said, "Pastor Teter, you need to pray for Junior." I introduced myself, and we bumped fists. He was a parent of one of Kara's classmates, and he looked like he was really struggling. I thought he might have the flu. I asked Mrs. Lipiz what was going on.

"Pastor Teter, you need to pray for Junior. He has stage four cancer. He is really, really scared." Then she ducked back into her classroom to begin the day for twenty kids. Right there in the kindergarten hallway of Webster Elementary, I laid my hands on Junior and began to pray. My hands began to get physically hot. I felt the presence of the Lord in our midst, and I prayed Psalm 50:15, declaring that today was the day of trouble, and we needed Jesus to rescue Junior. I also asked for full healing in Jesus' name. Then I was silent so he could communicate with God.

I asked him how he felt. He said that he felt better. I continued to pray and blessed him in the name of the Lord. We exchanged information, and he thanked me for praying for him.

That afternoon, I got the backstory from Mrs. Lipiz. Junior had testicular cancer. He was originally from Arizona but had come to Los Angeles because he couldn't find proper medical treatment in his community. The cancer had spread throughout his body, even into his lymph nodes. He was thirty-three years old and had two small children. And he was understandably scared.

I didn't see or hear from Junior for ten days. When I got off a flight to work on leadership development concepts with our church planters in Hong Kong, I turned on my phone in the airport. The first text was from Becky. She said I needed to call Junior immediately. He had left a message for me as well. I also had texts from three other people saying I needed to call Junior. God had moved, and the word was getting out.

While I was traveling, Junior had gone in for the results of his barium test. His testimony is that after waiting for "like four hours" in the Harbor UCLA Medical Center waiting room, his oncologist finally called him in. There was a team of doctors in the room, and they told him, "Junior, we don't know what to do." He told me that he thought at that point he was a dead man walking. He thought the cancer had become so aggressive he would die in a few days.

But the doctors pulled out their x-rays, charts, and tests, and said to him, "The cancer is gone."

The 72 are given power over demons and sickness. The power gifts are given to display supernatural power, which authenticates the message that we preach. As one of the 72, may you move in power and heal the sick in your community.

HABITS OF THE 72: TEACHING THE WORD TO NON-CHRISTIANS

Teaching the Scriptures is a ministry skill we all must develop. The apostle Paul encourages the young pastor at Ephesus, Timothy, to continue in the hard work of ministry, exhorting him, "For this reason I remind you to fan into flame the gift of God, which is in you through the laying on of my hands" (2 Timothy 1:6). As our friends experience healing, they come to us for teaching. Below are habits that will help you become a stronger teacher of God's Word.

- *Teach with authority.* Lead your friends into the Scripture as one who is sent by God. Live out 1 Peter 4:11 by speaking as one who teaches the very words of God.

- *Mentor.* Pick a few master teachers, preachers, and Christian communicators, and learn from their ministry. In today's communication age, there is great access to the core passages of the Bible. Choose a mentor as a ministry mentor.

- *Content.* The teaching goal with your non-Christian friends is that they understand the gospel so they can commit to following Jesus. I would recommend a seven-week series: Genesis 1–3; Luke 4–6; and John's Gospel: The Seven Signs. John's Gospel: The Seven Signs explores Jesus' miracles in John 2:1-11; John 4:46-54; John 5:1-9; John 6:16-21; John 9:1-41; and John 11:1-44.

- *Teach in the four learning domains.* Teach so that all four learning domains are covered: cognitive (information), affect (heart), volition (will), and experiential (life practice).

- *Use popular culture.* Our non-Christian friends live in a world that many Christians know little about. I would recommend you venture out into popular film, television, and sports to connect the Word to "current life" themes.

- *Go twenty miles.* D. L. Moody said he would walk twenty miles for a good illustration. A good illustration puts today's flesh on the core truth of the Scripture. Our friends today will know the Scripture is true because it really works. Most master teachers I know keep an ongoing file of illustrations.

- *Pastoral cards.* At the end of a study, pass out index cards. I ask my students to write down a question they have about God and a pastoral issue/prayer request for any current challenges or issues. I'm always amazed at how honest, desperate, and open people are.

CONVERSION CONVERSATION 3: FROM
CURIOSITY TO THE CROSS

The third conversation that every 72 witness must become competent in is the call to conversion. At this point along the conversion timeline, the gospel is taking root in the heart and life of the unbeliever. He is hearing from God in the Scripture, applying what he is learning in faith, enjoying fellowship with believers, and hopefully has seen God answer his biggest questions. John Stott, who considers the pursuit of God after his soul as a major part of his conversion, wrote, "My faith is due to Jesus Christ himself, who pursued me relentlessly even when I was running away from him in order to go my own way. And if it were not for the gracious pursuit of the hound of heaven I would today be on the scrap-heap of wasted and discarded lives."[1]

At this point in the conversion process, non-Christians grow in their awareness of Jesus' presence in their lives and in their hope in his promises. They're ready to begin following Jesus.

I hold to the ministry philosophy of private and public conversion in a local church context. While I believe in the work of the Spirit for conversion through public preaching, I've seen too many public amens not translate into strong disciples. If a person is not fully processed, an early commitment can put internal and external pressure on the convert. At FOL, I like to meet with new converts before their public commitment. Those that are starting their new life in Christ need this private meeting to understand the theological implications of conversion, count the costs of discipleship, and have a clear, personal discipleship plan for the first ninety days. The plan we provide for our new disciples emphasizes inner-life growth, personal devotions, and serving in ministry teams.

In 1952, an anesthesiologist named Virginia Apgar developed a five-point test to evaluate the effect of the birthing process on newborns. Today the Apgar test is a universal tool for the medical community to evaluate the health of newborns. In the same way, our church uses a modified version of the Apgar test to evaluate the spiritual health of new disciples. The converts are given a "spiritual Apgar evaluation" as homework, and they're encouraged to tell everyone they know that they are now following Jesus. (Seventy-two training can't begin early enough.)

Conversion Conversation 3 ends with a prayer of commitment. I read Luke 15 over the new disciples and pray that Jesus will fill my new sister or brother with the Holy Spirit. After this private commitment, they're encouraged to make a public commitment at our next Sunday service that includes a public proclamation at a harvest event. (FOL hosts four evangelistic harvest events each calendar year.)

Because of our three conversion converstaions, our friends have officially transferred their citizenship from the kingdom of darkness to the kingdom of light.

In August 2016, Fernando and Maria Jimenez and their three boys, Fernando Jr., Richard, and Vincente, became disciples of Jesus. Our friendship started through Little League and moved from the diamond to the Bible study. After three months of learning and living the Word of God, the Jimenez family was ready for this conversation. Here is Fernando's testimony of his conversion process and of starting his life in Christ with a clear call to faith.

FERNANDO JIMENEZ

I remember meeting John at a Little League baseball game. He would stand at the back of the backstop and make videos of the kids. After a few games, he introduced himself as a pastor. I was surprised because I always expected a pastor to be in a suit or to be a certain way. He was wearing an Orioles jersey and Kobe Bryant shorts. He invited me to church, so I told him "Sure, I'll send the kids."

I've never been too religious and didn't feel part of any religion growing up. On the Sunday when it was time to go to church, everyone got ready except for me. But I felt left out. So I started going every Sunday. I also began going to a weekly Bible study. We were studying the Gospel of John. After a few months, something clicked. I decided that I was on the right path. I hadn't realized that it was what I needed, but I knew it was time. I began going to church for the kids, but I realized that what was happening was not just for the kids to learn about the Bible. I was learning it for myself.

When I came to FOL, I saw that it was multiracial. I really believe that this is what our church is all about. I've always been a person who likes to help out, and the church allows me to do even more, because it's on the west side of Long Beach, and there sure is a lot of need. I'm proud because my son Fernando also decided to get baptized and get involved with church.

After a few months, Maria and I had a meeting in Pastor John's office. We had committed to following Jesus in the small-group Bible study a few days before, but we didn't really know what that meant. I'm usually a very cautious person, but this felt completely right, so I decided to follow Jesus. We mapped out the fall and how we could pray, learn more of the Bible, and serve with the church. I had heard stories before, but something was happening to me. My wife says I'm different. I'm less anxious, happier, and more peaceful.

I always love to bring people—relatives, neighbors, anyone I can ask—to church. When I talk to people, especially my neighbors, they are surprised because I never talked about church before. Any chance I get, I bring it up. Jesus is what people need, but they just don't know it yet. It's part of our job to get them in there.

SAMANTHA CARROLL

The fall of 2009 was a very lonely, sad time in my life. I had recently graduated with my master's degree (in painting and drawing), and I was teaching part-time at a bunch of different colleges. Because I was adjunct and living alone, I wasn't really close to anyone—just driving from school to school then collapsing at home at night.

My grandmother had died earlier that year after a long struggle with Alzheimer's disease, and I still felt deep grief over her passing. We had been close, and I visited her every week, but as her mind shut down, it was practically a relief when her ninety-one-year-old body gave out as well. Luckily, I still had a few friends from grad school; of these, my favorites were Andy and Jenny Dickson.

Andy and I had quickly become friends while attending [the] art program. We had both separately taught ourselves how to paint with pastels and were excited to meet someone else to talk with about pastels. Andy tracked me down in the halls, introduced himself, and then took me home to meet his wife, Jenny. Something just clicked when I met Andy and Jenny. Besides talking about pastels, I enjoyed Andy's humor, and Jenny's love for nature and hosting. The three of us had quickly become very good friends and were still in contact with each other in the fall of 2009 (five years after graduate school).

The only bad thing about being with Andy and Jenny was they were *constantly* inviting me to their church. I had been

raised Catholic but had lost my belief in God as I had grown
up and seen and experienced different hurtful things. God
seemed like a fantasy some people believed in. I didn't. I loved
being with Andy and Jenny, but I wasn't interested in joining
their church (which I told them again and again). However,
Andy got crafty. He invited me to his church again, but he
insisted it was only to help with an art project. He was supposed to do a large mural on the wall and asked me to help
him, or at least check out the wall and walk him through the
process. (This was plausible because Andy is a landscape artist
who paints small- to medium-size paintings. I am a figurative
artist who loves doing large work.) I, in such a barren emotional place, reluctantly agreed, but I told myself I would go
to this church only once.

The first time I attended Fountain of Life Covenant
Church was a mixed experience. I saw a really bad mural,
some type of collage of material representing animals. Andy
indeed had his work cut out for him; the existing art was bad,
and the wall surface was worse (bumpy, glossy stucco). The
music in the church was also strange; it was very different
than the Catholic hymns I had grown up with. However, the
pastor was different. He spoke about a loving God and how
God was a servant who loved meeting our needs. I reluctantly
started to listen. I wanted to learn more about this God and
his plan. At the time I felt rootless, like I was just drifting
from one experience to another.

So I went back the next week. And after that, I went back
again and again. In fact, I have never stopped coming since
that first day. Through going to FOL I learned about a different God than I had ever known—a God who is a loving
father, but who also gives us freedom to make our own

choices. I went to Barnes & Noble and bought my own Bible (who knew there were so many Bibles!) and then started reading it, so I could learn for myself. I literally fell in love with this God.

After some time, I thought I should probably join a Bible study. I am an introvert, and although I enjoy people, I rarely get close to many. (Andy and Jenny are the exception, along with a very few others.) I was not excited to go (to be honest, that is an understatement), but the pastor constantly stressed the need to be part of a life group. Eventually, when my schedule let up (that is, when I couldn't make the excuse about work anymore), I again reluctantly agreed. Months earlier someone named James Carroll had randomly invited me to his study, so I decided to go when my schedule was (unfortunately) freer. At my first meeting of James Carroll's "Upper Room" Bible study, people tried to explain what Bible study is like. "It's like Disneyland," someone said. "You enter in, and the rest of your life falls away. You are in a magical place for a few hours." I just looked longingly toward the door.

Eventually I did find that description to be right. Although I had to force myself through the first-hour dinner part, the second hour of studying the Bible passage became a very special time in my week. I was eager to read the passage and see if people really did believe and live this way. Through the group I met people that really did try to follow and live out the Bible. There were people present who had lost jobs yet still insisted on tithing, and people who had moved to different parts of the country in order to follow the Bible more closely. The same God amazed us all, but these were people who were living this out. I slowly started to see the value of community within my introverted world.

It has now been eight years since I first walked into Fountain of Life church. During these eight years, I have moved to the west side of Long Beach, started a ministry for children within a Section 8 housing program, helped to create a Bible study/art program for local children, and surprisingly married James Carroll, the man who invited me to Bible study. I'm daily amazed by God's goodness and plan. He really is alive. And he loves me. My life of faith has begun.

Today Fernando, Maria, the Jimenez boys, and Samantha are some of the strongest lay ministers in our church. The conversion process is now complete. The converts have moved from being curious to carrying the cross. The mission field will now be trained to become part of the mission force. May we thank God for his gracious will.

And may we rejoice that our names are written in heaven.

NEXT STEP: Please visit folantioch.org/resources for the "Antioch Academy Class: 72"

FEATURED RESOURCE: The Seven Signs of Jesus (Evangelistic Bible Study Series)

FEATURED RESOURCE: The New Birth Spiritual Health Inventory

CONVERSION:
REJOICE WITH ME

*Everybody thinks they are a beast. Until it is
time to do what real beasts do.*

BRIAN STEWART

This past Christmas, our friends Michael and Amber Chang invited us to present the gospel story for an inner-city outreach that their foundation was hosting in Santa Ana, California. Thirty middle school children packed into a community center. The Chang Family Foundation had provided an Olive Garden dinner, Christmas presents, and even a gingerbread house for each child.

Michael opened up the event with the icebreaker "What is your favorite sport?" Most of the children said soccer and baseball. He told them that his favorite sport was tennis. The children gave a blank look. They had never heard of the French Open and had no idea they had a champion in front of them. As our children ran circles around the jungle gym, we shared a laugh that we were all getting old.

The Christmas message I prepared for the children centered on why Jesus, the Son of God, became human and took on flesh—basically, God's party in heaven is so important, he wanted to deliver the invitation in person. Moments before I was going to speak, the staff worker for the youth center approached Michael and me and said in a stern voice, "Pastor, this is not a Christian ministry, so please make sure you deliver a Christmas story that isn't religious." I honestly didn't even know if a nonreligious Christmas message existed. I chuckled, asked Michael what he thought, and he said, "Well, I think we need to preach the gospel."

To honor the youth worker's request, I opened up my message with this line: "Hey, kiddos, facts are our friends and the facts are that God became one of us."

During the message, one of the youth raised his hand and asked, "Pastor, are you saying that if we believe in Jesus, we can go to heaven?" I was about to answer when the youth worker jumped in and told the boy, "You believe whatever you want to believe."

That afternoon in Santa Ana, I thought of the evangelism trends due to multiethnicity, postmodernism, and our post-Christian culture. The world is changing. Youth-center employees demand pastors deliver nonreligious Christmas messages to children. While the youth worker was not the giant computer-generated grizzly bear that mauled Leonardo DiCaprio in *The Revenant*, he was a reminder that the 72 are sheep among wolves. And I fear that as our postmodern and post-Christian culture matures, the wolves will only get bigger, stronger, and more dangerous.

Jesus never said that being one of the 72 would be easy. But he did promise we will have joy.

CHAPTER THEME: There is great joy (and pain) in the 72 lifestyle.

CORE TEXT: Exegesis of Luke 10:17

The seventy-two returned with joy.

The word *joy* in the New Testament Greek is *chara*, which means "delightful happiness." Though it's the grittiest, most challenging—and in some ways scariest book of the four Gospels—the theme of joy is present throughout the book of Luke. There is joy over John the Baptist's miraculous birth (1:14). The baby in Elizabeth's womb leaps as Jesus in Mary's womb enters the room (1:40). The angels are filled with joy as they proclaim Jesus' birth in a star-filled heavenly choir (2:10). There's joy when we're persecuted, because of the great rewards (6:23). Angels rejoice when lost sons and daughters come home to the Father (15:7). And the disciples return "with great joy" to Jerusalem after meeting with the resurrected Jesus, the firstborn of the new era of humanity (24:52).

As we've worked our way through the calling, training, and sending of the 72 (Luke 10:1-24), I hope this flow of joy rising up in the text has been your experience as you've learned about and tried to live like the God who loves sinners. Consider this extended quote by Jonathan Edwards on the centrality of joy in God:

> God is the highest good of the reasonable creature. The enjoyment of him is our proper duty; and is the only happiness with which our souls can be satisfied. To go to heaven, fully to enjoy God, is infinitely better than the most pleasant accommodations here. Better than fathers and mothers, husbands, wives, or children, or the company of any, or all earthly friends. These are but shadows; but the enjoyment of God is the substance. These are but scattered beams; but God is the sun. These are but streams; but God is the fountain. These are but drops, but God is the ocean.[1]

The third gospel is full of joy. For a world so dark and devoid of happiness, an evangelist that is full of joy is an amazing apologetic.

Luke 15 is a partner chapter to Luke 10. The theme of witness and joy is present throughout the three parables of lost people, animals, and precious heirlooms. When the Shepherd brings home the lost and vulnerable sheep, because of his joy, he throws a party. When the woman finds the lost ring that is part of her future dowry and inheritance, she also calls her friends and neighbors and hosts a party. When the lost son returns from reckless and soul-damaging living, the father runs to him, kills the fatted calf, and throws a party. There is also a repeated exhortation in the chapter: "Rejoice with me!" (15:6, 9). The command of God to his people, especially in the area of evangelism, is to rejoice with him in the amazing work of rescue.

But how do we seize this fleeting joy in our broken world? And how do we live into this joy as we seek to be faithful and fruitful witnesses under ever-increasing pressure? I believe there is joy to be gained in our daily evangelism habits.

DAILY EVANGELISM HABITS

As Christians, we love to read the inspiring accounts of Luke 10 and the great deeds of the 72. Our hearts burn within us when we read the account of the church exploding in Jerusalem. The apostle Luke wrote that the teachings of the church filled the ancient city where Jesus was falsely accused, executed, and raised from the dead by the Father. We read multiple accounts throughout Acts of the Lord adding to the numbers of the church daily.

But I have yet to hear a sermon or an extended teaching on how this actually happens. It's almost as though we put on mystical lenses and chalk up daily evangelism growth to some indefinable movement of the Holy Spirit. But could daily growth in the church be more connected to the discipleship of those who love Jesus?

In our own lives, we believe in the concept of doing things daily. We're incredibly limited and finite creatures who need food and water daily. To operate properly, our Great Designer has humbled us, and we can't function properly without eight hours of daily sleep. We brush our teeth daily. We sing to our young children and help them get ready for bed daily. The list can go on and on and on.

In Luke–Acts, we find more than a few daily commands and requests. We are to deny ourselves, take up the cross, and daily follow Jesus (9:23). Jesus teaches us to pray for our daily bread (11:3). The disciples saw Jesus teaching in the temple every single day (19:47). The first church created a system of daily distribution of bread to widows in need (Acts 6:1). The Bereans were declared noble because they were committed to studying the Scriptures daily (17:11). Paul evangelized in the hall of Tyrannus every day for a time (19:9).

Could it be that the Lord added to the numbers daily because his witnesses shared their faith daily? If we take off the religious lenses that overspiritualize conversion, we see a basic premise of giftedness development. The 72, and all of the New Testament evangelists that followed, saw daily conversions because they were faithful witnesses every single day.

It makes perfect sense. We go to work at our jobs every day. We feed our children daily. Many of us try to pray daily. Why would we not be kingdom workers working in the Lord's full harvest every single day?

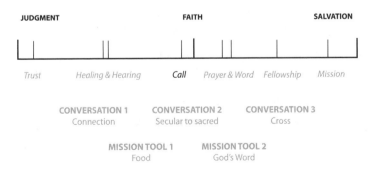

Figure 8.1. Conversion process timeline

TRAINING TAKEAWAYS

A few years back I suffered a serious knee injury. Michael Chang was very gracious to connect me to his trainer, Coach Ken Matsuda, for my rehabilitation. In the 1960s, he coached the USC track team, and he pioneered core training, resistance-band strengthening, and nutrition concepts. Coach Ken applied these principles to tennis and for close to twenty years helped Chang win thirty-six Association of Tennis Professionals tournaments and hold the world's number-two ranking for over seven years.

Coach Matsuda and his wife, Jan, are wonderful Christians and amazing people. For over forty years, they've been faithful members of Rolling Hills Covenant Church, the grandparent church of FOL. I was allowed into the "Matsuda Dojo" upon Michael's recommendation, because Coach Ken has a soft spot for the over-forty-year-old pastors with bad knees. Working out in the Matsuda Dojo taught me four training lessons that apply to being the best version of the seventy-two evangelists we can be.

1. *Preparation meets opportunity.* The 72 were ready when the door of opportunity opened. We can never predict when an eternity-altering moment will present itself. As evangelists, we must be ready in season and out of season. I shudder to think how many incredibly thoughtful, specifically designed, grace-filled evangelism opportunities God has prepared for us, but we were not ready. The 72 must master the fundamentals of personal evangelism so we will be ready for every evangelistic opportunity.

2. *Can't* means *won't.* I was on the mat, and coach was instructing me how to do a medicine-ball core exercise. I tried to do it, but my body would not respond. I looked at him and reported, "Sorry, Coach, but I can't do that exercise." He quickly replied, "No, you can do this exercise, but you're choosing not to. *Can't*

means *won't*." For the next month, I worked hard and was eventually able to master the exercise. The 72 don't stop at *can't*. Too often we stop because of the pain. We must push through *can't*.

3. *Someone is working harder.* If we are to reach elite levels, we must dedicate ourselves to hard work. There's no shortcut to mastering a sport—or, in our case, personal evangelism. I'll never forget Coach telling me about the work ethic of one of his players. He put the player through a grueling two-hour band workout in the morning. The player then put in four hours of on-court drills. Then they said good-bye and agreed to meet the next morning to do it all again. But that evening, there was a knock on Coach's door. It was the same player, asking Coach for an evening workout. Coach told him to rest, relax, and go home. But he said, "No, I need another workout. Someone in the world is working harder than me right now." The 72 know evangelism is very hard. We also know that somewhere in the world, the devil is working very hard. It's a choice to work hard on our craft and our call to personal evangelism.

4. *One hundred times in a row.* The goal in our evangelism training should be delivering excellent ministry every day. I will never forget standing next to Joe Chang, Michael's father, watching a club tournament player. He hit an amazing running forehand up the line for a winner. His shot drew many oohs and ahhhs from the tennis club crowd. His opponent even shook his head. I commented to Mr. Chang, "Wow, he is a really good player." He replied, "But John, can he do that one hundred times in a row?" Being one of the 72 is not a one-time shot or a great moment. We must train to create ministry habits that bear fruit daily.

I pray and lift you up to the Lord of the harvest. May you apply some of these training principles to praying with earnest power, making spiritual friendships, and helping your friends experience the healing of God and the Word of God.

"YOU ARE ONE OF THE 72"

I end *The Power of the 72* with a personal illustration that means a great deal to me. As I have reflected on Luke 10:1-24, I believe this personal experience captures the joy (seeing God move and bring a friend to faith) and the pain (of rejection) of living out the vision of the 72. We must remember that Jesus spent seven verses teaching the ministry skills of evangelism and seven verses talking about rejection.

On one particular evening, I took Kara, our four-year-old daughter, with me to put "being one of the 72" into practice. We walked up and down our block, inviting numerous neighbors to our study. Kara, with her super-tight Shirley Temple curls, is cute as a button and was handing people the Life Group flyer. How could anyone say no to Kara? I like to call her my "secret 72 weapon."

Kara and I first came to a young man who was getting out of his car. We had met a couple of times before, and I knew he was living with his girlfriend. He knew I was a pastor, so I knew that I caused him to feel a bit uncomfortable. For this encounter, I wanted to connect with him about popular culture, so we chatted about the Lakers. It was a nice connection. Then I gave him an invitation to play some basketball with friends from church. I asked for his phone number and entered it in my phone. I then told him I would call him so he would have my number.

Later I dialed it, but his phone never rang. So he had deliberately given me a wrong number. We had exchanged an awkward fist bump, and I wanted to crawl into a hole.

On our forty-five-minute ministry tour around the neighborhood, this happened two more times. I was zero for three. I was feeling hurt, discouraged, and tired. But that's to be expected. As I walked home with Kara, I explained to her that the witnesses of Jesus aren't always treated as nicely as they should be.

We were two doors away from our home when we ran into our neighbor, Joanie. She works very hard and is not very available. Most of our interactions are brief waves while pulling out of the driveway. I decided to walk over and invite her to the small group. I began our conversation by asking about her boyfriend, and she told me he was a loser and was now serving four years in prison. She had a new man whom she loved very much, and they were five months pregnant. We wished her well and told her how happy we were for her. I then asked her if she wanted to come to the Bible study. Joanie actually showed excitement and said, "I'll be right over."

As we studied the Bible that evening, Joanie was very engaged. We were in our fifth week of studying Luke 10:1-24. She loved the passage and shared openly about how it was the first time she had been in the Scriptures since she was ten. Her aunt had taken her to a study, but had been diagnosed as being bipolar and was in a mental institution; she had suffered some terrible traumas. But Joanie said, "I really remember liking the Bible studies as a child."

After the study, while everyone was having snacks and making small talk, I asked Joanie what she thought about the study. Her face got very serious. She asked if she could share a personal need. Earlier that week, she'd had the big five-month ultrasound appointment and had received a call earlier that afternoon that her baby had two of the five soft markers for Down syndrome. She was terrified. She then shared that at four that afternoon, she had stopped and prayed, saying, "God, please be with me and send me help."

She looked up with tears in her eyes and said, "And then he sent you to me, and here I am, studying the Bible."

I brought her over to Keva Green, one of the amazing disciples that serves on staff with FOL, and together we opened our mouths and laid out the gospel for Joanie. She was able to identify how God was breaking into her life. She said she wanted to follow God and was more than willing to make the sacrifices that were required by faith in Jesus. Keva then invited her to follow him. We prayed for her as she began her formal relationship with Jesus in our living room.

As we finished praying, Joanie looked up at me with wonder on her face. She said that it was amazing how the Bible study had come alive and how she saw her own story in the text. Then she said words that I will always remember and embrace as a divine affirmation from God.

"John, this is just like the Bible. You are one of the 72!"

Epilogue

A FINAL BENEDICTION

Evangelism is not easy. But Jesus trained the 72 for witness, and all thirty-six teams returned with joy.

Suffering, pain, and rejection do not have the last word in evangelism. In the kingdom of God, the way up is down. If disciples are to save their lives, they must be committed to losing their lives daily.

Luke dedicated much writing to evangelism and Jesus' all-out search for lost sheep, lost coins, and lost sons. The process is painful, but the rewards don't compare with the afflictions. There is only one command in the fifteenth chapter of Luke. As the Shepherd invited his disciples into his own commitment to evangelism, he exhorted, "Rejoice with me, for I have found my sheep that was lost." Joy awaits in the midst of the pain of sacrificial ministry.

Jesus gave power to seventy-two ordinary disciples for extraordinary evangelism.

The 72 prayed. The 72 developed spiritual friendships. The 72 helped their friends experience God's healing and hear the Word. And the 72 called people to faith.

You also are one of the 72.

Together, may the Spirit empower us to do what the 72 do.

Go and do likewise.

ACKNOWLEDGMENTS

Evangelism is all about people. In the same way, a book about evangelism is about people who share the faith, people who follow Jesus, and all the wonderful people behind every ministry. No book happens in a vacuum. If there is an encouragement or a ministry insight that blesses you in this book, the following people are likely responsible. I thank God for their friendship and investment in my life.

Evangelical Covenant Church—I learned so much about national leadership serving our denomination in evangelism and church planting (2010–2016). Thank you to Dave Olson, Gary Walter, Dick Lucco, and Fredrik Wall for the opportunity to lead evangelism and church planting. I thank God for our mission friendship.

FOL Antioch Church plants—It is a great joy to bring mentoring encouragement to younger church planters. I love being a Barnabas to these young Pauls: John Perkins in Jackson, Mississippi; Andrew Morrell in Marion, Indiana; David Washington in Chicago; Michael Thomas in Seattle; Simon and Millie Yeung and Reverend Tam in Hong Kong; Grant and Miho Buchholtz in Tokyo. May you all develop as urban apostles and finish well.

FOL—Where did ten years go? Thank you for your faith, love, service, and commitment to West Long Beach. You make church planting and pastoring a joy. God has given us an amazing evangelism learning lab. Thank you for all of your faith and hard work.

Landon Yoshida—Why didn't you convert after my broken-racket gospel presentation at USC? The Lord's timing is perfect. What a joy to see you and Miko become *ohana* for the FOL family. *Mahalo!*

Ryan Mallari—Thanks for being such an inspirational ministry partner and shrewd manager of kingdom resources, and for laughing so hard at all of my dumb jokes. The dream is becoming a reality.

Paul and Holly Liu-Dutra—So glad God reconnected us through Yelp! I will always remember the Reiber Hall lemonheads, our original snack wall. Becky and I love learning, laughing, and building the kingdom with you.

Doug Schaupp—I am so thankful for your faithful prayers, patience in hearing twenty years of confessed sin, and wise counsel.

Alex Gee—Twenty years ago we "accidentally" met among the 17,000 students at the Urbana Student Mission Conference. Only God knew what a great mentor and friend you would become in our lives.

Jeff and April Hanson—The lines have fallen in pleasant places: second-grade friendship, Psalm 23 and the Halliburton Road car chase, D7 turning into FOL, and planting churches all over the world. It's been amazing to see God's plans for two lost sinners from the Heights. We can't wait for the 2040 Simeon Farewell Tour.

John Tumminello—Thank you for helping us clarify the call, live out the vision, and mix in a salad and buy a cup of coffee. I love your faith, your learning posture, and our friendship. Thanks for embracing the call to be one of the 72!

Isaac Flores—Thanks for being the best friend a pastor could have. So glad you and Katie decided to come back for a second service ten years ago. Your music and leadership are such gifts to FOL. We are just getting started, Ike Bryant.

Bobby Clinton and Darrell Johnson—The apostle Paul said that while we have many leaders, we only have a few fathers (1 Corinthians 4:15). Thank you, Bobby Clinton and Darrell Johnson, for your mentoring and discipling in our lives. What you've taught Becky and me has made all the difference in our life and ministry.

Tim Sato—Jesus teaches that the greatest in the kingdom is the servant of all. We will all be lining up behind you, brother. I thank God for how you develop your wonderful ministry gifts, your tireless work ethic, and the amazing way you "take care of everything and all of us." Bravo, Uncle Nim Nim!

Carol Sato—Thank you, Mom, for being an amazing kingdom worker. You are a gifted administrator and evangelist, steering FOL and FOL Antioch, and sharing your faith with many. I thank God for our life together and the mission partnership that extends from our home in West Long Beach all the way to Asia.

Joy, Kara, and Luke—You three are such great gifts from God. Each of your births is full of God's goodness and drips with destiny. I love my front-row seat to watch Jesus' grace upon grace roll out in your lives. Daddy loves you, but always remember that Jesus loves you most of all.

Becky—In 1999, God told me that you are my "good wine." After seventeen years, you have become such a powerful leader in the kingdom of God. Thank you for creating new ministries like the Family Center and 5000 Pies. You inspire us with your fruitful evangelism and discipling. And somehow you keep all of the chaos at bay with an unmatched work ethic, poise, and humor. You are truly amazing. Today, I testify that you get better with time! I love you, Becky Teter.

NOTES

INTRODUCTION: WELCOME TO THE POWER OF THE 72

[1]Darrell W. Johnson, *Experiencing the Trinity* (Vancouver, BC: Regent College Books, 2002), 69.

[2]Peter Thiel, *Zero to One* (New York: Crown Business Books, 2014), 3.

1 FAITH COMES FIRST

[1]Jonathan Edwards, *The Life and Diary of David Brainerd* (Boston: Yale University Press, 1985), 157.

[2]Joel Green, *The Gospel of Luke* (Grand Rapids: Eerdmans, 1997), 276.

[3]J. Robert Clinton, *Focused Lives* (Altadena, CA: Barnabas, 1995), 1.

[4]Darrell Johnson, *Discipleship on the Edge* (Vancouver, BC: Regent College Publishing, 2004), 57.

[5]Peter Scazzero, *The Emotionally Healthy Leader* (Grand Rapids: Zondervan, 2015), 17.

[6]Fred Bergen, compiler, *The Autobiography of George Mueller* (London: J. Nisbet Co., 1906), 152.

[7]Darrell Johnson, *Fifty-Seven Words That Change the World* (Vancouver, BC: Regent College Publishing, 2005), 92.

[8]Quentin Tarantino, *Pulp Fiction: A Quentin Tarantino Screenplay* (New York: Hyperion, 1994).

[9]Thomas Smail, *The Forgotten Father* (Grand Rapids: Eerdmans, 1981), 11.

2 SENT TO THE POOR

[1]Martin Luther King Jr., "Remaining Awake Through a Great Revolution," sermon delivered at the National Cathedral, Washington, DC, on March 31, 1968, https://kinginstitute.stanford.edu/king-papers/documents/remaining-awake-through-great-revolution.

[2]G. Campbell Morgan, *The Gospel According to Luke* (Eugene, OR: Wipf and Stock, 2010), 22.

[3]Joel Green, *The Gospel of Luke* (Grand Rapids: Eerdmans, 1997), 102.

[4]E. Stanley Jones, quoted in William Barclay, *The Gospel of Luke* (Philadelphia: Westminster Press, 1956), 9.

[5]Kenneth E. Bailey, *Jesus Through Middle Eastern Eyes* (Downers Grove, IL: IVP Academic, 2008), 147.

[6]David Bosch, *Transforming Mission* (New York: Orbis, 1991), 98.

[7]John Perkins, *With Justice for All* (Ventura, CA: Regal, 1982), 107-8.

[8]Dallas Willard, *The Divine Conspiracy* (San Francisco: Harper Collins, 1998), 40.

[9]Curtiss DeYoung, et al., *United by Faith: The Multiracial Congregation as an Answer to the Problem of Race* (New York: Oxford University Press, 2003), 2.

[10]Wendy Thomas Russell, "Trouble Spot in Long Beach: Four Gangs Operate in West Side Apartment Complex," *Long Beach Press Telegram*, November 15, 2003, www.streetgangs.com/news/111503-long-beach.

3 WOLVES, BEARS, AND CRUSHING PRESSURE

[1]From lyrics by Jay Z and Alicia Keys, "Empire State of Mind," *The Blueprint*, 3 Roc Nation Records, 2009.

[2]Darrell Johnson, *Discipleship on the Edge* (Vancouver, BC: Regency College Publishing, 2004), 67.

[3]Joel Green, *The Gospel of Luke* (Grand Rapids: Eerdmans, 1997), 360.

[4]William Barclay, *The Gospel of Luke* (Philadelphia: Westminster Press, 1975), 136-37.

[5]Jonathan Edwards, *The Life and Diary of David Brainerd*, ed. Norman Pettit (New Haven: Yale University Press, 1985), 207.

[6]Ibid., 278.

[7]Ibid., 370.

[8]John Piper, "Oh, That I May Never Loiter on My Heavenly Journey," sermon delivered at the 1990 Bethlehem Conference for Pastors, Minneapolis.

4 HOW PEOPLE BECOME CHRISTIANS

[1]E. Stanley Jones, *Conversion* (New York: Abingdon Press, 1991), 15.

[2]John E. Teter, "Discovering and Constructing New Models of Evangelism Leadership" (doctoral dissertation, Bakke Graduate University, Seattle, 2012).

[3]Doug Schaupp and Don Everts, *I Once Was Lost* (Downers Grove, IL: Inter-Varsity Press, 2008), 31.

[4]John Teter, *Get the Word Out* (Downers Grove, IL: InterVarsity Press, 2003), 128.

[5]David T. Olson and Craig Groeschel, *The American Church in Crisis* (Grand Rapids: Zondervan, 2009), 67.

[6]Schaupp and Everts, *I Once Was Lost*, 11.

[7]Olson and Groeschel, *American Church in Crisis*, 68.

[8]Ibid.

[9]Ibid., 69.

[10]Darrell Johnson, *Discipleship on the Edge* (Vancouver, BC: Regency College Publishing, 2004), 21.

[11]Olson and Groeschel, *American Church in Crisis*, 77.

[12]Soong-Chan Rah, *The Next Evangelicalism* (Downers Grove, IL: Inter-Varsity Press, 2009), 181.

[13]Takeshi Takazawa, personal interview, 2013.

5 EARNEST AND POWERFUL PRAYERS

[1]G. Campbell Morgan, *The Gospel According to Luke* (Old Tappan, NJ: Revell, 1931), 135.

[2]Darrell Johnson, *Fifty-Seven Words That Change the World* (Vancouver, BC: Regent College, 2005), 21.

6 FRIENDS: SECULAR TO SACRED

[1]Craig Keener, *The IVP Bible Background Commentary: New Testament* (Downers Grove, IL: InterVarsity Press, 1994), 216.

[2]David T. Olson and Craig Groeschel, *The American Church in Crisis* (Grand Rapids: Zondervan, 2009), 177.

[3]Keener, *Bible Background*, 216.

[4]Jan Martinez, *Christ's Kitchen: Loving Women Out of Poverty* (Sisters, OR: Deep River Books, 2013), 33.

7 EXPERIENCE: HEALING AND HEARING

[1]Roger Steer, *Basic Christian: The Inside Story of John Stott* (Downers Grove, IL: InterVarsity Press, 2010), 262-63.

8 CONVERSION: REJOICE WITH ME

[1]Jonathan Edwards, *The Works of Jonathan Edwards*, vol. 2 (London: Banner of Truth Trust, 1974), 244.

ALSO BY JOHN TETER

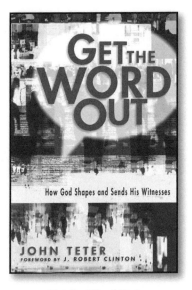

Get the Word Out:
How God Shapes and
Sends His Witnesses
978-0-8308-7532-0